What You Need to Know About Taxes

...and Federal spending
...and the National Debt
...and the National Monetary System

I0482133

Charles Layne

What You Need to Know About Taxes
Copyright © 2017
Charles R. Layne

Printed in the United States of America
First Printing, 2017

Author:
Charles R. Layne
FLFIRST500@AOL.COM

Printed in the USA by:
CreateSpace.com

Front Cover: The IRS Building, Washington, D.C.

Contents

Appendices

List of Figures

Preface

The title of this book is a very tall order to fulfill. Many tomes have been written on and about these subjects. The proliferation of books and articles on the subject of money and monetary systems is due to the many vantage points from which the subject can be viewed. Everyone knows what you can do with money but beyond that, for many people, things get murkier.

How and who creates money, how banks operate, the role of the central bank, how the quantity of money in the economy is managed, etc are all interrelated parts of the monetary system picture that are not well understood by many citizens.

I strive in these pages to provoke the reader to think and consider facts about money, taxes, government spending and the national debt. My goal is to have the reader more informed and more confident of his or her knowledge of these subjects and to have immunity from the prolific misinformation often seen in the media.

I have tried to make the facts easy to understand and I have included historical documents to illustrate and support the facts that are presented.

Our money system and tax system are old,

based on the infrastructure we had a century ago. Our present monetary system is an artifact of the "gold is money" era while we are using a fiat money system started by FDR in 1933. We live now in a new age that offers new insights into the nature of money and new tools to provide the processes needed to manage the nation's money supply.

I describe in these pages how these new insights and new technologies can be used to rid ourselves of the shortcomings of our present, antiquated system that failed us so resoundingly in 1929 and again in 2009, causing great pain and suffering here in the USA and around the globe.

This book reflects two and a half decades of my avocational interest in the subjects of monetary theory, banking and the fiscal affairs of nations. My interest in these subjects was instigated by an article in USA Today in the early '90s. The article noted that for the first time ever federal government borrowing from banks exceeded borrowing from banks by the private sector. Coming from a physical science background, I was dumbfounded by the article; I did not know the federal government borrowed nor needed to borrow from banks.

Being aware of my ignorance on the subject I

turned first to Federal Reserve publications and learned a lot from them. I contacted my congressman and he introduced me to a senior analyst in the Federal Reserve. He was very helpful in explaining basic facts about the Federal Reserve and the monetary system.

A book I highly recommend for neophytes on the subject is John Kenneth Galbraith's well written, often amusing and always very informative book entitled "Money Whence it came, Where it Went", John Kenneth Galbraith, 1975, Houghton Mifflin Company.

Two computer programs are available with the purchase of this book. One is a data base program that displays graphic and textual data on monetary, banking and demographic information. Email the author for a copy of the programs.

Graphical illustrations are used throughout the book from this program. The second program is an interactive tax system tool.

I have learned a valuable lesson in writing this material. In trying to organize the material into coherent parts I found myself repeating myself because the elements of our monetary and fiscal systems are so entwined. It is difficult to talk about one part without commenting on the other parts. It is a characteristic of the subject that makes it difficult to understand as well.

When you find repetitions understand that the subject sometimes requires it to explain the entwinement of the elements of our monetary and fiscal systems.

First US Bank
1791 – 1811
120 South Third Street
Philadelphia, PA

Chapter 1

Money: What is it? [1]

The subjects discussed here, taxes, debt, banks and the Federal Reserve, have one thing in common; they all involve money. That makes it worthwhile to look at the nature of money, what it is and what it does for us before getting into the details of these subjects listed in the title of this book.

We use many things in our daily lives and, for the most part, we know what the things are AND we know how we can use them. And we don't confuse how we use them with what they are. For ex-

---

[1] Chapter 1 is an excerpt from an essay written by the author at an earlier date. The complete essay is included in Appendix D

ample, a cell phone: We know it is made from metal, plastic and has electronics in it and that it uses radio waves from a tower someplace; that is what it is but we use it to talk to people (and sometimes computers) who are far away from us. It is the same with a car; it is made of metal, plastic, rubber and wires; it needs a battery and we have to pump in fuel but we use it to go from point "A" to point "B" if there is a passable road between the two points.

What a thing is and what we use it for are two totally different things. But, unfortunately for us individually and perhaps our society as a whole, there is one thing we use on a daily bases with which we have trouble conceptualizing the difference between what it is and how we use it. Money. We are taught from the time we are toddlers what we can do with money. Ask anyone out of the blue "Do you know what money is?" and they will probably smile and say "Of course." But then press them with "Well, what is money?" and they might frown, think a little and then respond, "Well, you can buy stuff and pay bills with money." Right. That is how you use it. Now, what is this money, totally divorced from how you can use it? That's a much harder question. Many noteworthy people have commented on this basic ignorance about what money really is. Henry Ford made a famous comment concerning money. He said: "It is well enough that people of the nation do not understand our banking and money system, for if they did, I believe there would be a revolution before tomorrow morning."

I agree with the observation of another wise but controversial person, Ezra Pound, who opined that the social consequences of the world population fully understanding money would compare with the experienced consequences of the world population generally becoming literate, which were, as we all know, truly enormous.

The literature is replete with good articles and books on money, what it is and how our current monetary system evolved. These books, articles and observations stretch back from the present day to near pre-history. Even Jesus is quoted as giving an insightful observation when he advised someone to "give unto Caesar what is Caesar's and unto God what is God's", noting that money is really the property of the state; that we are only using it.

We can start our quest to understand money

by considering why there is such a thing as money. Why was it needed? How did it come into being? A real hermit would not need money. Living alone and out of contact with other people he would never need nor have an opportunity to use money. Likewise, a very individualistic and conservative person who can build his own shelter, provide for his own food and make his own clothes would not have a real need for money. He would only need money if he wanted things or services provided by others.

From these observations we can see that money is coupled with living with other people, living in a community and depending on others to provide some parts of our needs while we, in turn, supply some of the needs of others. Money, then, is the enabler of a collective society where people depend on each other to supply their needs and diverse desires. A "collective society", as I use the term here, is merely one where people depend on the labor of others to satisfy their needs and desires.

In fact from all that we know about man and his evolution through pre-history, we have always been a collective society. Even cave man had his artists who ate, lived and thrived while someone in his collective group provided him food and shelter. Hence, it is fair to say, we as humans cannot conceive of a society that is not a collective society, where people depend on the labors of others to provide some of their needs and desires while, in turn, they also provide to others using their own capabilities.

Over the past decades another evolution we have seen has been the increased diversity of things we depend on others to supply to us and for which we use money to secure. A century and a half ago the important things requiring money were very limited compared to the highly diverse things and services now available in the market place. This increased diversity of commodities and services acquired with money obscures the basic function and original need for money. We can fail to see money as a tool to enable us to live with others and depend on them for our needs and, in turn, their dependence on our own productive work to supply something of value to them.

If we accept the notion that money is the enabler of a collective society where people depend on each other for their livelihood requirements then we do make money a commodity with ethereal qualities. How many movements, rally's, speeches, inspirational courses and organizations have the objective to achieve a society where people depend on each other and care for each other? Could we say every religion we understand and perhaps those we do not fully comprehend have as a goal "the brotherhood of man" and respect and service for others? Could it be that this stuff we call money is the key to attaining these lofty goals proclaimed by noble persons throughout history? An admonition about money well known to us is given in First Timothy 6:10, "For the love of money is the root of all kinds of evil." And it can be; but it does not have to be.

Accepting the arguments above regarding how money is used and what it does for us as a society, we still need to address the question, "What is money?" The simple answer is that money is a bartering commodity with a widely accepted value. It simplifies the bartering process with the buyer having a commodity of accepted value to exchange for the sellers commodity or service at the price offered by the seller. Money simplifiers the bartering process by requiring only the buyer to evaluate the value of the offered item rather than both parties having to evaluate the value of the item offered by the other.

The simple definition of money given above does not address how money is created and issued or how it is distributed into an economy. It is these aspects of money that are murky and confusing in the minds of many.

A part of the confusion is there is no single, simple answer to these questions. There are multiple vantage points from which to view each question and there are additionally many different ways in which money is created, issued and distributed. A well known economist, Hyman Minsk, pointed out in a humorous way a very important aspect of these issues. He pointed out that it is easy for anyone to create money. The real problem is getting it accepted as money with value.

Imparting value to a new, first issue money is very different from maintaining value of money that is and has been in circulation for an extended period of time. The money issued by the Virginia colony shown in appendix B illustrates how initial value can be imparted to the issued money. First, the colony required taxes and fees to be paid with the newly issued money, providing an incentive for all to acquire enough to satisfy tax obligations. The act also made the issued money redeemable for Bank of England specie or coin, established money with recognized value. In other words, the colony money was "backed by" English coin.

The Department of Economics at the University of Missouri–Kansas City has developed the Modern Monetary Theory school of thought, considered a leading voice in current economic thought. They teach that the government, by requiring taxes to be paid in the money issued by the government, imparts value to the money. It is obviously a strong teaching but there are other factors which influence the value of a money. One is the simple question, "What can you buy with the money?" This, classically, has related to the productivity of the economy in which the money is used. In this era of vigorous international trading, it brings up another point, what can be purchased internationally with the money.

The US dollar is a good case in point. With the US dollar you can buy oil and every nation must have oil and every nation must secure dollars to buy oil which is priced on the world market in dollars.

The pricing of oil in dollars is not an accidental fact. It is the result of the long standing relationship between the Saudi family in Arabia and OPEC plus the USA's hegemony over the mid east, the major producer of oil. Recent military actions in the mid east can be viewed as actions to maintain hegemony there and to maintain the world oil market in dollars.

An ancient approach for money creation, and one still supported by many, is to depend on nature to supply money by using gold as money. Supporters of "gold as money" believe money should have intrinsic value and not just symbolic value. Coins have been minted and are currently being minted from gold here in the USA and gold certificates have circulated as money (pre-1933) where the certificates were redeemable for an amount of gold specified on the note.

The problem with gold as money is that a growing economy and population requires more money than nature supplies. The Federal Reserve Act of 1913 partially fixed that issue by allowing banks to issue four gold certificates for each unit of gold they had in reserves; i.e. the reserve requirement was twenty-five percent. That worked well until the great crash of '29 was followed by people descending on banks demanding gold in exchange for their certificates. Thousands of banks were forced to close because they did not have the gold to satisfy the holders of gold certificates. FDR ended the chaos with his famous executive order shown in Appendix C which closed all banks and changed the nation's monetary system from gold backed currency to fiat currency as we have today. The dollar retained its convertibility for gold internationally under FDR's order but that was ended in 1971 by Nixon when he removed gold backing for international exchanges too, making the dollar a true fiat currency.

Our nation has had many monetary systems over the years. The Federal Reserve is the third central bank in the US. The first two lasted only for the duration of their original charters; twenty years. The Fed is over one hundred years old and is chartered now in perpetuity and can only be disbanded "for cause." It was, however, created by the congress and can be modified or disbanded by the congress. In the following chapters the features and details of our monetary system will be discussed and examples will be shown illustrating how the system can benefit the citizens of our nation.

Second US Bank
1816 – 1836
420 Chestnut Street
Philadelphia, PA.

Chapter 2

The Monetary System

Our monetary system creates money and supplies it to our economy. The system includes the Bureau of Engraving and Printing (BEP), a part of the US Treasury that prints all paper currency and bonds sold by the Treasury. The mints, also a part of the Treasury, produce US coins. These facilities of the US Treasury furnish coins and currency to the Federal Reserve Banks for distribution through commercial banks to clients in accordance with their desire for cash.

Coins furnished to the Fed from the mints are added to the Treasury's account at the face value of the coins without reference to the cost of production of the coins. Dimes and quarters cost less to mint than their face value; they have a positive seigniorage. Both pennies and nickels cost more than their face value to mint, having a negative seigniorage.

Paper currencies, Federal Reserve Notes, produced by the BEP are "sold" to the Federal Reserve for the cost of printing. A $100 bill costs the Fed fourteen (14) cents.

The Treasury, and thereby the citizens, enjoy the benefits of the seigniorage on coins but not on paper currency. To understand how citizens benefit from coins, take the example of quarters produced by the mints. In 2016 2,356,030,000 were produced with a face value of approximately 589 million dollars. However, the cost of minting the coins, just under 9 cents per coin, was only 212 million dollars. The seigniorage was 377 million dollars or the government was able to spend 377 million dollars for goods and services for the American people without borrowing the money or balancing it with tax collections. This is an extremely important point. The federal budget can be balanced with seigniorage in addition to tax collections and borrowing. This fact is not shown on the balance sheets.

The banking system enjoys the benefits of the much higher seigniorage on paper currency or Federal Reserve notes. Banks do not enjoy the seigniorage directly, i.e. they do not issue the currency by buying things. Instead, they issue the notes through loans and thereby draw interest on the seigniorage. Most loans never end up as cash. Transactions using credit only suffices in most of the economy.

This difference between the nature of paper currency and coins means we have, in actuality, two separate and distinct monetary systems, one for coins and one for paper currency. In the end, both monetary systems support the credit system on which the majority of the economy functions.

Coins are fundamentally different from paper currency. Coins are sovereign money, minted by the government under powers granted by the constitution. The Federal Reserve notes, issued through banks by loans is often designated "debt money" because someone had to be in debt to a bank in order to have the money in the economy.

If you were to ask someone to describe how a bill in there wallet got from the Treasury's BEP printing presses into their wallet they would probably have great difficulty explaining the process. Tracing it backwards might be hard but if we start at the BEP it is easier to understand. All Federal Reserve notes printed by the BEP are shipped to and stored in the vaults of the twelve Federal Reserve banks. In exchange, the Federal Reserve credits the US Treasury's spending account with the cost of printing the notes.

Every commercial bank has an account at its regional Federal Reserve Bank. A commercial bank can, when they have a need for cash, draw down their account (called their reserve account) and have cash delivered to them, the cash becoming their vault cash. It is important to remember that every Federal Reserve note follows this path. There are no exceptions.

In order for that money in the bank's vault to get into the economy as new money, someone must make a loan with the bank and take the proceeds in cash. If someone comes to the bank with a check drawn on another bank and gets it cashed, no new money has been created. That money was already in the economy and has just been moved from one location to another. The bank on which the check was drawn has to pay the bank that cashed the check by transferring funds between their reserve accounts. The Fed cleared the check by transferring the funds and the bank that cashed the check has the money in their reserve account replacing the cash paid out from their vault cash. This process is called "check clearing."

Coins are not the only example of sovereign money spent by the federal government. The government does not borrow coins or sovereign currency such as US Notes that had the red serial numbers, and silver certificates as issued until the late 60s.

The most notable historical example of sovereign spending was under Lincoln when his "green backs" were used to pay for the Civil War when bankers were asking for interest payments as high as 36%.

Over the past few decades sovereign spending has been drastically reduced. The issuance of silver certificates ended after JFK was assassinated. The spending of US Notes was stopped in Jan of 1971. Dollar coins were minted but never circulated. Recently, minting of the half dollar coin was ended. Currently, both the penny and the nickel cost more to mint than their face value. The only US coins producing positive seigniorage are the dime and quarter.

Chapter 3

The Money Supply

An economy without money is called a barter economy. It is a very slow and ponderous economy with "deals" always very difficult to make. It is obviously not an ideal economy. On the other hand a government/our government could print money and spend it into the economy, paying people to do things and buying things from people. If this process is followed inflation will eventually occur. As money continues to accumulate in the economy prices will rise and money saved by citizens will become less valuable. That process, printing and spending money, is neither a proper nor sustainable process.

Two very important lessons can be learned from these very brief and simple observations. First, when a government spends money into an economy it must then remove some of the money to prevent the detrimental effects of inflation. This removal process is called taxation which removes money from an economy, making room for more spending by the government. This is the basic function of taxes; to remove and destroy money previously spent into the economy, thereby preventing inflation.

Many people, including politicians, will tell you the government "needs" tax money in order to operate, and they tell you and teach you this untruth because they want you to believe the government must adhere to a budget as a responsible housewife[2] must do. They have a reason to convince you that the government is budget limited by taxes. They do not want the government providing you with services you need; they want those services performed by the private sector at a profit. And that is all well and good if the private sector can and will supply those needs. However, in many

---

[2] They do not mention that the housewife must have a machine which prints legal money to make the comparison accurate.

cases, the private sector cannot or will not provide the needed services and then the fallacious concept of budget limitations hurts all of us.

We have many examples now in our society of needless suffering caused by the untruth that budget constraints prevent providing needed services to people. Three overwhelming examples are health care, education and national infrastructure. We lag behind developed nations in all of these areas because of the lie about budget constraints. In each of these cases resources are more important than money. The government cannot buy nor furnish that which does not exist. We are probably resource limited in both health care and education which means the government should be supporting expansion in both of these areas.

There is no excuse for allowing our infrastructure to become so outdated and dilapidated. We do have the resources to repair and build the infrastructures we need to enhance our economic and social lives.

Considering the process outlined above, government printing and spending money into an economy then removing a part of what was spent to prevent inflation and maintain the value of the money, a curious bookkeeping fact is discovered. Since the government does not take back all the money that it spent- which would be quite stupid to do- then the amount of money in the economy is equal to the national debt! And "money in the economy" includes the money in your pocket!

The Colony of Virginia's Money Act, March 1760, shown in appendix B, discusses this detail of spending and removal of spent money. This fact was well understood over 250 years ago! The act requires an accounting of the redeemed money, just as we do now, but is very specific in requiring the redeemed money to be "...burnt and de-stroyed."

Taxes are not needed as income to enable spending by the government in this era of fiat money. This point was made clear in 1946 by **Beardsley Ruml who, at that time, was Chairman of the Federal Reserve Bank of New York. His paper is shown in appendix A. Money became free to the federal government in 1933 when FDR ended the era of gold backed currency, replacing it with the fiat currency that we now have.**

The second important lesson from our basic considerations is that there must be an optimum amount of money in an economy, somewhere between none and an inflationary amount. The problem is determining and maintaining the "optimum" quantity of money in an economy.

A method proposed by bankers was chosen in 1913 by the Congress and incorporated into the act that established our third central bank, the Federal Reserve. The motivation to establish a new monetary system was very intense and real, fueled by the bank panics in 1907 and the national confusion resulting from many banks printing their own money, certificates that were, supposedly, redeemable in gold.

During negotiations between bankers and a few senators, a method was established which is now called an endogenous money supply system which means growing from within or let the market determine the amount of money in the economy. That sounded like a good approach then as it does now. Even today it has very broad support in the economics community.

Our endogenous monetary system is not difficult to understand. There are two parts to the process, how the government is constrained in fiscal matters and how banks operate making loans.

First, the federal government is prevented from either adding to or subtracting from the money supply[3]. That is done by "balancing the books" with government spending being constrained to equal the sum of taxes destructively extracted from the economy plus funds borrowed by the US Treasury.

The borrowed amount is called the deficit.

This bookkeeping process neuters the power of the government to add money to or remove money from the economy.

Many argue that government deficit spending is a stimulus to the economy and they are correct. The "stimulus" does not come from adding money to the economy. The government borrows idle money that people want to save and not spend nor invest. The government then, by spending it into the economy, converts it to active money flowing in the economy. The process does increase the national debt which will be discussed in a later chapter.

Banks provide all money to the economy with

---

[3] Exceptions are coins, silver certificates that were spent under JFK, and US Notes with red serial numbers that were spent until 1971. These are/were minted/printed and spent into the economy without borrowing.

a few exceptions. Those exceptions are coins and paper currency such as "greenbacks", US Notes (with the red serial numbers) and silver certificates. All of these paper currencies were printed and spent by the government without borrowing or obtaining them through taxing.

Lincoln printed and spent greenbacks to pay for the civil war when banks were asking for interest rates as high as 36% to loan funds for the war. They were used from 1861 to 1865. US Notes had a longer life, from 1862 until 1971. Silver certificates were issued from 1878 to 1964. The only paper currency currently issued by the US Government is Federal Reserve Notes, produced by the Bureau of Engraving and Printing (BEP), given to the Fed and then used, as needed, for backing bank loans and for the cash requirements of payees of government spending.

Commercial banks provide loans as demanded by actors in the economy. The process is very simple but not widely understood. Let's say you need to borrow $10,000 to purchase equipment for your small business and that you have collateral and are creditworthy. Only two things happen, other than the signing of papers, when you make the loan. The loan officer will go to the computer and access your account. Then he or she will increase the amount in your account by $10,000 using the computer keyboard. That is a liability to the bank. They now owe you $10,000 more than they did before making the loan. Then they post a new asset; that you owe them $10,000. The books balance and $10,000 has been created out of thin air. Now you can use your $10,000 to buy your equipment which removes the bank's liability. The bank has paid out the money they loaned to you. When you pay off the note the bank's asset disappears. The $10,000 is no longer in the economy. It disappears but the bank keeps the interest you paid. The process is so simple it boggles the mind but that is the way it is done and that is our endogenous monetary system.

The first part of the scenario above, the creation of the funds out of thin air is easy to follow but the disappearance of the money at payoff is not so obvious so let's look at it in another way. Let's suppose you need cash to make the purchases. You will then, after the loan is consummated, write a check payable to yourself for the amount of the loan and the bank gives you cash out of their vault. You walk out of the bank and suddenly realize you do not need the money so you turn around, go back in the bank and return the money and that money goes back into the vault where it was before. Everything is now as it was before the loan was made except for the early repayment penalty the bank might charge and the minimum interest that accrued on the loan. The 10k created out of thin air by keystrokes has disappeared from the economy. It no longer exists.

This is the system we have that creates money by making loans and the money created disappears when the loan is repaid. The process is often called the way banks put money into the economy. There is, however, another vantage point. Every successful bank loan results in money being taken out of the economy by the bank. This aspect of banking supports the conclusion of many that banks do not create money but only rent temporary access to money for a fee called interest. Another description of the process is that they extend temporary credit.

The endogenous money supply system failed in the aftermath of the '09 crash because banks stopped making loans and, people who could, paid off their loans thereby reducing the amount of money in circulation. That caused deflation which in turn resulted in a loss of jobs, reduced demand for products and caused foreclosures on homes for the simple reason that not enough money was in the economy to pay the money due on outstanding loans.

Classical economics taught that the amount of money in a market economy did not alter anything. The assumption was that prices would adjust to whatever quantity of money existed and therefore economists could ignore banking and the monetary system in general when studying markets and employment.

A criterion for an optimum money supply is now well known and broadly accepted. That criterion is that the money supply should maintain price stability and full employment. The congress offloaded the chore of maintaining a proper supply of money onto the central bank established in 1913, the Federal Reserve. The dual mandate of the Fed is to maintain price stability and full employment, full employment being defined as an unemployment rate between 5.2 and 5.5% and price stability being defined as an inflation rate of 2% per year.

The Fed failed on both counts prior to and in

the aftermath of the '09 crash. Figures 1 and 2 show the CPI has been growing at a rate near 3.7% per year and that the most complete measure of unemployment, U6, shows an unemployment rate peaking in the aftermath of the crash at over 16% and currently at 10%.

Some will tell you the reasons for the failure of the Fed is a complex issue but, if you back off and look at it, it is simple. The Fed does not have the tools to control both inflation and employment. The classic tool used by the Fed has been the Federal Funds interest rate.

The Federal Funds Rate is the rate charged for bank to bank overnight loans. The Fed reduced this rate to essentially zero but banks still did not make loans and the money supply did not grow. The other classic Fed tool is buying and selling of the national debt, and yes, that is one basic need and function of the national debt. When the Fed buys a piece of the national debt, money is placed in bank reserves enabling banks to make more loans. Alternatively, selling the debt removes mon ey from reserves, reducing the ability of banks to make loans. Due in no small part to the Fed's QE programs and the national debt buying spree in the aftermath of the '09 crash, bank reserves became enormous but still loans were not made and deflationary pressures continued.

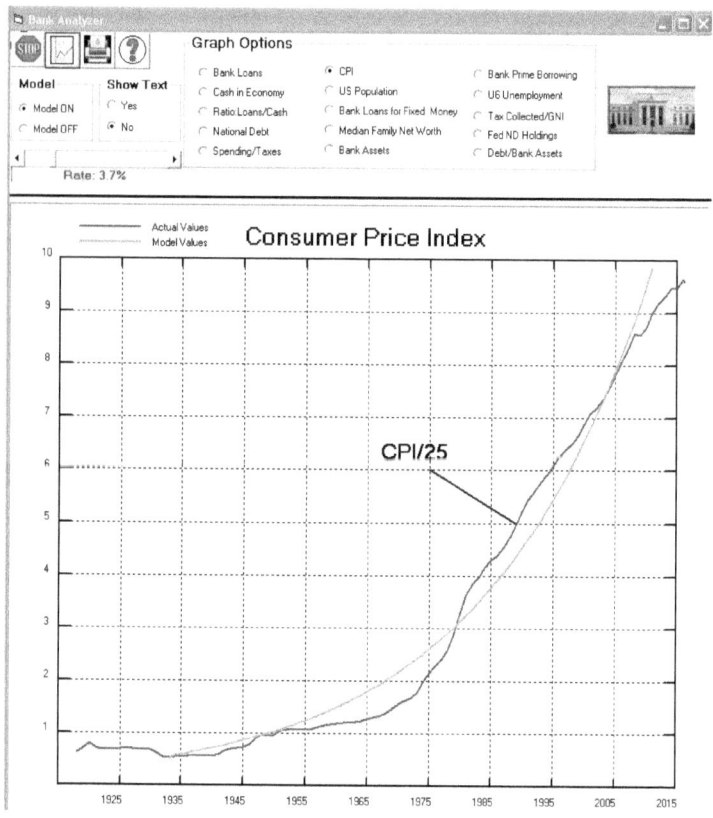

Figure 1 Consumer Price Index

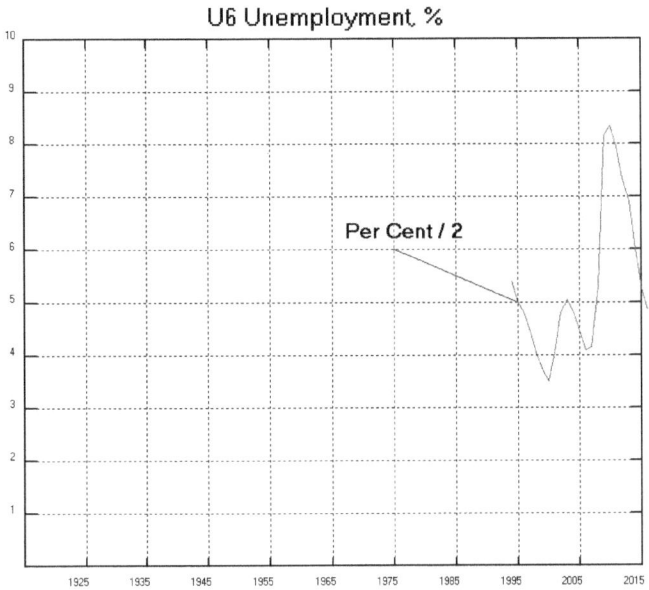

Figure 2: U6 Unemployment Rate

Our monetary system failed us and our government failed us. We did not have to experience the pain so many suffered after the '09 crash. We could have had a rapid recovery but politics got in the way and that politics was fed by the general ignorance of the citizenry of how the national monetary system can work for the benefit of the citizens.

The Fed failed us because they do not have the tools to fix the problem other than Bernanke's "helicopter" money, flying a helicopter around and dumping money out for people so they will have money to buy things, increasing demand and putting people back to work producing stuff for them to buy.

The congress did not fix the problem because the status quo, a "liquidation" phase as Andrew Carnegie described it in 1929, is good for the 1% and the 1% holds a majority in the congress.

When the quantity of money in the economy decreases the prices of assets go down. People are forced to sell their assets to obtain money, depressing prices by supply being greater than demand. This is the time when those with money can buy assets at low prices, thereby increasing their wealth. That is what happened in the aftermath of the '09 crash. In the aftermath of the '09 crash the mean net worth of American families was cut almost in half as shown in the Figure 3.

Many people struggle to understand the monetary system while others just ignore it. The subject is not taught in secondary schools nor will

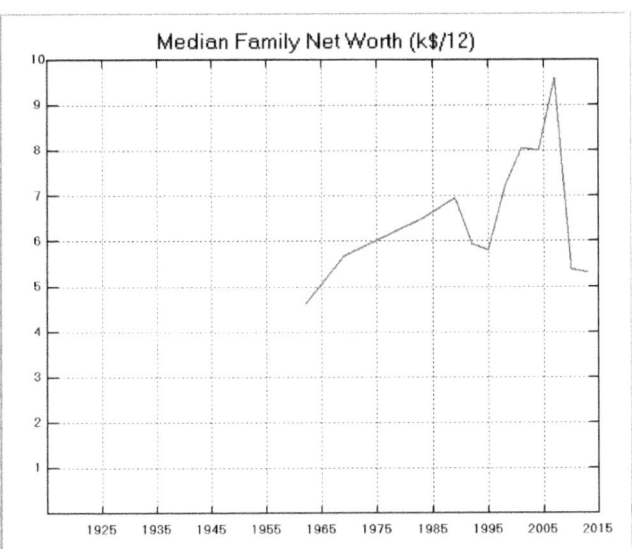

Figure 3 Family Net Worth

you be exposed to it in college unless you choose to study economics. Even if you study economics you may not be exposed to the monetary system if your school's economics department holds to the precepts of classical economics which teach that the money supply is meaningless and can be ignored in the study of markets.

An allegorical story illustrates the features of our current fiat monetary system. A father with teen age children decides to teach his young children about the real world and introduced them to some new family rules. They were assigned chores and when they completed them they were paid by family money created by the dad. In turn they had to pay in family money for their room and board, movie tickets, etc. The project worked, the kids did their chores, and got paid, paid their way and saved some money too, using it among themselves to buy things from each other. A family economy was established. The father, when he got paid back with his money did not have to save and store what came back. It was easier to trash the money and make new ones than to store the old ones.

That is how our fiat money system works except we redeem excess money as taxes rather than for room, board and movie tickets.

There is another difference, a more profound difference. Suppose the father in our scenario decided he was not competent to control the amount of money in his family economy and enlisted help from a next door neighbor who was very smart in money matters. He and the neighbor agree the father will only spend the amount of money he collects for services he provides his children plus an amount he can borrow from them, removing his power to alter the amount of money in his family economy.

In return his neighbor is given the power to create money for the family and loan it at interest to any of the children who need additional funds. You will probably think the father would be silly to follow this course but if he did then it would be a very precise replica of our monetary system with a central bank and privately owned commercial banks creating money in the economy with loans.

Chapter 4

The National Debt

The national debt is a political football and many unfounded things are preached by some about the debt. Understanding it is not hard to do. First of all it is a necessary tool for our central bank, the Fed. As a tool of the Fed, the debt must increase as the economy expands and the population of the nation increases. The Fed buys the debt to put money into the economy and sells debt to remove money from the economy and from commercial bank reserves to lessen their ability to make loans. Additionally, the Fed, under law, must hold debt as backing to Federal Reserve notes that it holds.

Secondly, the national debt serves as a very safe savings account for individuals and organizations with large quantities of idle cash. The safety of saving money with the federal government is the reason the Treasury can sell bonds while paying very low interest rates. The alternatives for people/organizations with idle cash would be to invest it or spend it or put the money in a bank where it is not safe.

There are many people who do not want you to understand the national debt. They only want you to think it is "big" and they want to keep you ignorant to serve their purposes. Their purpose is usually described as their desire to have a small government but that translates to their desire to block the government from providing services all citizens need in order to allow private corporations to sell those same services at a profit.

Let's look at how the size of debt should be determined. Self-serving economists like to divide the debt denominated in dollars by the GDP denominated in dollars per year which gives an answer denominated in years which no one can explain.

Most people will look at debt in a very simple way. If you are in debt for $5,000.00 and you only have $50.00 to your name then you have a big debt that is 100x your fiscal assets. On the other hand a person may have a debt of $1,000,000.00 but have assets of $10,000,000.00 so his debt to asset ratio is 0.1 making the million dollar debt a small debt.

Now, is the 16T$ national debt really big if we view it in this manner? To get an answer we need to determine the fiscal assets of the federal government. To understand the issue we can look at how the national debt is paid as it becomes due, and some part of it becomes due almost every day. Once upon a time, before the Internet, when a Treasury bond became due a check was written, signed and mailed to the bond holder. Now, however, with Internet communications available, it is much simpler and faster.

A computer program accesses the bank account of the person/organization that owns the maturing treasury and increases the balance in the account by the face amount of the treasury plus the interest. The program also loads the amount paid, principal and interest, into a data base of treasuries available for sale, and they will be sold.

That is all that happens. In this way the debt is rolled over continually and not a cent of tax money is ever used to pay principal or interest on the debt. Nor will your grandchildren ever have to pay it! Nor are we paying the debt incurred by our grandparents!

Bottom line: the fiscal assets of the US Federal Government are infinite and the debt to asset ratio is zero which is as small as it can get.   This does not mean the debt/savings account should be allowed to increase without limit nor does it mean the national debt is a good thing. It does mean that the debt is a choice of the federal government and it can be paid down at any time the government wishes to do so, an action that would cripple the Fed and take away a safe place for wealthy entities to save idle cash.

With the good, or at least tolerable, aspects of the national debt defined, we can look at the bad side and the unethical side. The bad side of paying off the national debt is that it would unleash, over a period of thirty years, 16T$ of money into the economy, potentially causing inflation. However, considering the source of these funds, large blocks of idle dollars, it is doubtful that many of them would end up at a Wal-Mart checkout counter. It would take thirty years, the term of the longest treasury that is sold, to pay off all of the debt. That would only be 533B$ per year which the congress should be able to deal with via taxing and spending.

A better way to deal with the money released by paying off the debt would be for the government to charter a National Savings Bank which would accept deposits from people with idle cash who do not want to risk it by depositing in a private bank. The bank could serve many other purposes as discussed later.

The other significant result of paying off the debt would be the crippling of the Fed, taking away its tool for management of the money supply, and thereby foisting that responsibility onto congress. That would be a gigantic political issue. It is very rational, however. Spending and taxing, the exclusive prerogatives of congress, are the natural tools for management of the money supply.

It is interesting to look at the record of the Fed buying and selling the national debt during the run up to the '09 crash and in the aftermath of the crash. Figure 4 shows the Federal Reserve holdings of national debt from 1970 to the present. From 1970 until early 2007 the Fed was increasing their holdings of the debt at an annual rate of about 3.7% per year (the green line), action that pumped money into the economy.

In mid and late 2007, prior to the crash, they sold debt, which takes money out of the economy. In 2009, after the housing bubble had busted, they went on a buying spree, pumping money into the economy, attempting, it would seem, to undo the damage they did by removing money from the economy. Their debt buying spree has not repaired the damages caused by the crash. We are still living with the scars of that crash to this day. Did the Fed serve us well? I think not.

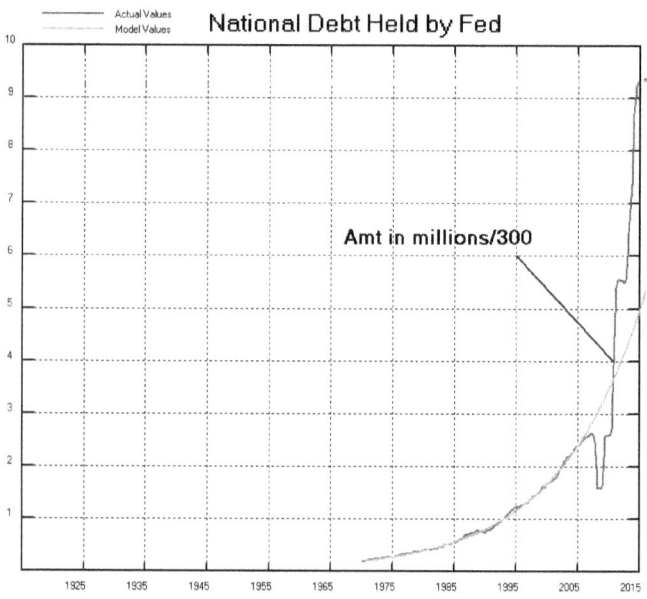

Figure 4: Fed's Holding of Debt

Finally, there is the moral issue associated with the national debt. The federal government is not allowed to change the actual quantity of money in circulation by the bookkeeping requirement that spending must equal the sum of taxes plus money borrowed by the treasury. Fiscal policy, therefore, does not change the amount of money in circulation but it does move it around in the economy by taxing A, borrowing from B and spending to C.

Noteworthy is that the borrowed money is usually idle or hoarded money. It is not being spent nor invested. It is not moving around in the economy; it is just sitting there as idle cash. The government then spends those funds and they become an active part of the economy which is beneficial to the economy.

The immoral part is that taxes, which balance the other part of federal spending, are not returned at interest to individuals as are the borrowed funds. Granted, federal spending should support tax payers as a group but as individuals, taxes paid are just lost.

Federal Reserve Building
Washington, D.C.
1913 -

Chapter 5

Banking and the Fed

Banking is probably the least understood business operation in the country. The conventional notion is that you need a lot of money to start and run a bank and, in fact, the membership fee is very high, $1,000,000.00 for your start up reserve account at the Fed. But once you open the bank people literally give you money. It is called deposits but when you deposit money in a bank you give legal title of the money to the bank. They just owe you the amount you deposited. The bank has legal title to the money.

Some people opine that banks are just like other businesses. They are not. Banks are very different in two significant ways. First, they create their "product" out of thin air. No other business does that. Second the "rental price" of their product is denominated in the same units as the product. You pay dollars to rent dollars. That would be like a grocery store renting a dozen eggs for 13 eggs or a car dealer renting you ten cars for a year for 11 cars.

Banking is very different from other businesses that produce products or provide services for a price in dollars, not in the units of the product or service they offer.

That is why usury, lending money at interest, has been condemned at one time or another by all religious groups including Judaism, Christianity and Islam. The difference is that Christian nations have embraced usury while Islam still forbids usury. This is an underlying base for the ongoing strife between Islamic nations and western nations.

The great economist, John Kenneth Galbraith, had a humorous way to describe the difference between banks and other businesses. Galbraith teaches[4] banks must spend money before they get it whereas other businesses have to get money first and then spend it.

Our central bank, the Federal Reserve, was formed many years ago in December of 1913. Many

---

[4] "Money Whence it came, Where it Went", John Kenneth Galbraith, 1975, Houghton Mifflin Company

things have changed[5] over those years. A massive change to the monetary system was made by FDR twenty years later in 1933, removing gold backing of domestic money. That was eighty-three years ago. Thirty-three years later in 1971 another significant change was made by Nixon, ending convertibility of US dollars for gold in the international arena. That was forty-five years ago.

Serious thought was given to the nature of our monetary system by many economists following the great crash in 1929. Two of three serious ideas that evolved were enacted into law. One was the separation of commercial banking, the process of making loans to people and organizations, from investment banking where banks seek to make money by investing in business enterprises. This separation of banking into two separate categories was enacted in the Glass-Steagall Act in 1933. Another was regulations of derivatives by the Commodity Exchange Act of 1936.

Notably, both of these regulations of banking

---

[5] See Federal Reserve summary of changes at: https://www.federalreserveeducation.org/about-the-fed/history

and stock trading were deactivated and decriminalized by Bill Clinton during the last year of his second term, earning for him significant responsibility for the crash in '09.

During the primary campaigns of 2016 Bernie Sanders called for reinstatement of Glass-Steagall and Hillary Clinton voiced her opposition to reinstating Glass-Steagall.

The third proposal made in the aftermath of the 1929 crash was never enacted into law. It was called the "Chicago Plan" and it was backed by many in the economic community. The Chicago Plan would have ended the ancient banking fraud of lending money they do not have, resulting in bank runs that have plagued banking for centuries. It would have ended the practice called fractional reserve banking. Bankers were and are vehemently opposed to such actions which would deprive them of their most significant power.

The Chicago Plan is far from dead in this era. There are a number of proposals on the table to modify the monetary system stimulated in no small part by our most recent crash in '09. One is focused on policy alone while others vary from subtle to massive in nature including one that has been described as the Chicago Plan on steroids.

Summarized below are the features of each. All are very well documented in the literature. The most conventional proposal comes from the Modern Monetary Theory (MMT) School of economics at the University of Missouri in Kansas City. They teach a new policy approach to the existing monetary system. They teach, correctly, that taxes destroy money and are not used to fund government operations. The benefits of deficits are also taught, that deficit spending converts idle cash to active cash in the economy.

A large quantity of material relevant to MMT teachings is available on the Internet and in published media. Their teaching that only policy adjustments are needed to "cure" the monetary system makes them apologists of the existing system. Noteworthy is the fact that two of the strongest voices for MMT, Dr. Stephanie Kelton and Dr. William Black, were picked as economic advisors for the Bernie Sander's primary campaign in 2016.

A second method is described in detail at www.realmoneyecon.org. The proposed approach is supported by many economists and by many in the Federal Reserve. The approach is a modification of the "Chicago Plan" first proposed in the 1930s as a measure to prevent future collapses such as the crash of 1929.

The center piece of the proposal is converting commercial banks into trust institutions that hold depositors money and can only lend actual money they possess, removing their power to create money out of thin air. This process would result in retiring the national debt over a weekend with some left over, making the US a creditor and not a debtor nation. The weakest issue in the proposal is how credit needed by the economy can be created if it is not done by banks. An approach is given in the web site material.

A third approach and the one that has proven itself in the real world, is Ellen Brown's proposal to establish public banks. One exists now in the USA, The Bank of North Dakota, owned and operated by North Dakota and created in 1919. It has been and continues to be a total success in the state, enabling the state to emerge unscathed from the economic storm of '09.

Ellen Brown has documented the benefits of this approach at publicbankinginstitute.org. This approach is very pragmatic. It does not alter the central banking system; it only changes how state and local governments and potentially the national government can beneficially change the way they deal with money, loans and deposits.

A fourth approach, the only one to receive significant media attention and to actually reach POTUS's desk, is the high **seigniorage** coins (HSCs) or multi T$ platinum coin proposal. Under the constitution congress has the power to "...coin money and set the value thereof..." Additionally, current law allows the US Treasury to mint platinum coins. The proposal is for the US Treasury to mint platinum coins with a face value of 10 or even 100 trillion dollars and place those coins in the Treasury's account at the Fed. Here is a quote from the site[6] listed in the footnote:

"What is useful in the platinum coin idea, and the central point of derision amongst protectors of the status quo is if taken to its logical conclusion, there is no need for debt—government could create and distribute as much money as is needed via pub-

---

[6] A discussion of the proposal can be found at: http://www.nakedcapitalism.com/2015/02/joe-firestone-return-platinum-coin.html

lic policies in the public interest.... "

The T$ coin proposal is very subtle in numerous ways. First, it plays on the seldom discussed fact that we actually have two separate and distinct monetary systems; one for coins and one for paper currency. Coins are minted by the US Treasury and placed in the Treasury's account at face value. The **seigniorage**[7] **of both pennies and nickels is negative;** the cost to mint them as of 2014 is greater than the face value. Pennies cost 1.66 cents each to mint and nickels cost 8.09 cents each. Quarters are minted for 8.95 cents, giving a positive **seigniorage.**

Paper currency, i.e. Federal Reserve Notes, are created by the US Treasure and then given to the Federal Reserve. The Fed only pays the Treasury for printing costs. A $100 bill costs (2016) the Fed about 14 cents! The seigniorage on paper currency does not directly benefit the American people as coin seigniorage does. If the money flow is analyzed what is found is that banks, by making loans on money created out of thin air, earn interest on the seigniorage of paper currency. This fact becomes

---

[7] Seigniorage is defined as the difference between the face value of a monetary instrument and the cost to produce it.

more obvious if you make a loan and take it in cash.

The T$ coins could also, over the long term, significantly affect Fed operations and congressional responsibilities. If 100T$ were added to the Treasury's account by minted HSCs then the Treasury would not need to borrow money, allowing the national debt to be paid off over a period of thirty (30) years, the longest term bond sold by the Treasury. This would put a burden on holders of large quantities of idle cash such as pension funds and wealthy individuals. The government should charter a National Savings Bank, as noted above, to provide the services lost by paying off the debt.

Additionally, the Fed would lose its most valuable tool for management of the money supply. Buying/selling the national debt to add/subtract money from the economy would no longer be a tool available to the Fed. The Fed could still set the overnight interest rates for banks and would still function as the national clearing house but the Fed would no longer be in control of the money supply in the economy. Congress, spending from the HSC assets, would be putting money into the economy that could not be removed by the Fed selling the national debt. Congress would need to step up and take responsibility for managing the money supply through spending and taxing, the natural tools for management of the money supply.

Very little is new under the sun with money. The government has often spent money into the economy without borrowing as would occur if HSCs were minted. The most noteworthy occasion of printing and spending was Lincoln and his green-backs which he printed and spent to pay for the civil war[8] after bankers demanded usury interest rates for loans. US Notes, the ones with red serial numbers, were new "greenbacks," printed and spent until 1971. The number of these was limited by congress just as HSC spending would be limited by the face value of the coins.

The challenge of HSC coins is providing a viable and acceptable framework for the destructive extraction of excess money in the economy, what we usually call taxes. The public and the congress would need to understand and accept the process. If successful the nation would be debt free and the citizenry would be better educated on money matters including the need and function of taxes.

---

[8] See Appendix J

Chapter 6

The Instability of Banks

History teaches us that banks are unstable. Fractional reserve banking, lending money they did not have, was blamed for the instability in the era of gold backed money. Central banks, acting as "lenders of last resort", were organized to come to the rescue of banks subjected to a run with depositors demanding money the bank did not have.

But now, in this era of not just fiat currency but also computer keyboard and computer program money creation, we have seen the instability again in 2008. Hundreds of banks failed in the aftermath of the crash. Most were small banks; the "to big to fail" banks were rescued by the Fed's QE programs.

How can this be? Why has our financial system failed in this era when money is easily created by responsible authorities? We are offered many explanations about overpriced derivatives, housing bubbles, credit default swaps, etc. to explain what happened but it is not at all clear which is the cause and which might be the effect. The verbose articles explaining the crash are not satisfying. They do not lead us to a place where action can be taken to prevent future occurrences of similar events.

The criminalization of derivatives and the passage of Glass-Steagall following the crash of '29 definitely helped stabilize the financial system in the decades between the '30s and the '90s. The de-criminalization of derivatives and killing of Glass-Steagall by Clinton in the late '90s did contribute to the crash in '09 but it is hard to blame it all on those two items.

The feeling remains that, lurking in plain sight, is some cause or some process which is responsible for the periodic crashes which have plagued banking systems over the ages.

It can be argued that there is such an issue, one we all see and think we understand but an issue that has the power to cause the crashes we suffer in cyclic intervals. It will be demonstrated with words and with mathematics that these cyclic crashes are an integral part of our banking system.

In her book, "Fighting Chance", Senator Elizabeth Warren quotes Jamie Dimon as saying "...a financial crisis every five to seven years is inevitable..." and then she states: "He was wrong." However, as much as I admire and support Senator Warren, I believe Dimon has a better grasp of banking than does Senator Warren. The Senator believes proper regulation can prevent crises but I see in the math of banking that crises are inevitable as Dimon said.

We must first define what a bank is and what it does. Commercial banks, collectively, are authorized by the federal government via the Federal Reserve System to be the sole source for individuals and other entities in the economy to obtain use of new money not presently in the economic system.

In the above sentence the word "use" is very important and significant in understanding bank operations. Banks do not "sell" money nor transfer ownership of money; they actually rent access to money for a limited period of time, the term of the loan. Moreover, the rental fee is denominated in units of that which is rented and, when the rental period expires and the loan is repaid then the money that was rented disappears.

This process is unheard of in any other part of an economy. Applying it to any other commodity in an economy is laughable. Who would accept renting ten cars for a year with the requirement of returning eleven cars at the end of the year with the ten rented cars being destroyed when returned? Renting something in units of itself is obviously fraught with unusual issues.

Consider the following block diagram of an economy served by a bank:

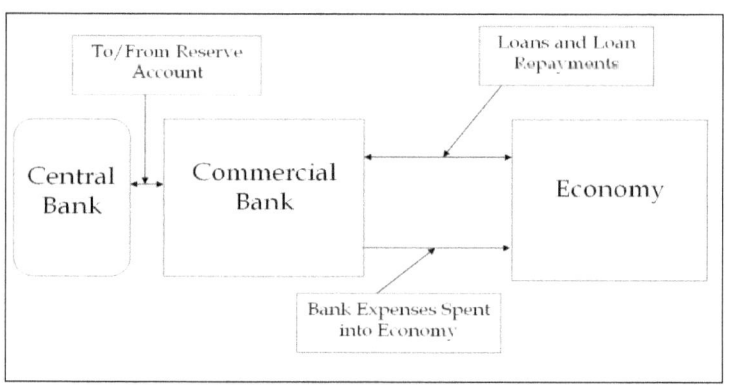

Figure 5: Bank / Economy Money Flow

The mathematical modeling is really very simple as is the math. It could be called a Gedanken experimental analysis and it is shown in Appendix E.

Assume a system defined by the two blocks, one block designated as the economy, consisting of all the elements of an economy; resources, agents, consumers and, a necessary condition for banks to function, a money supply which does not accrue interest by its presence in the economy.

We also assume the economy has undeveloped resources enabling it to grow. To the left of that box is a box labeled "Commercial Bank" connected to the economy with a double ended arrow line indicating a flow of money in each direction. We impute to the bank the capability to modify the quantity of money in the economy via loans made at a designated interest rate and for a designated term.

The interest paid by the borrower can be divided into two parts. A portion will represent the spending of the bank into the economy for salaries, supplies and dividends to stock holders.

The second part will represent the portion of the interest that goes out of the economy and into the bank's reserve account and thereby increases the wealth of the bank. This later rate defines the money extracted from the economy by bank loans.

We could add government to the system but it is unnecessary because the government can change the location of money in the economy by borrowing from "A" and spending to "B" but cannot alter the quantity of money as long as the rule spending minus taxes must equal treasuries bought/sold by the US Treasury.

The government can cause transient changes in the quantity of money in the economy but this, from the viewpoint of a systems analysis of the quantity of money in the economy, can be characterized as noise which will have no long term effects.

The additional arrow from the bank to the economy indicates a flow of money into the economy from the bank. This flow is the cost of operation of the bank from using labor and resources from the economy plus payment of dividends.

To perform a mathematical analysis one must state assumptions and initial conditions. Two assumptions are made. First, it is assumed that commercial banks, as a group, can be modeled as a single bank performing the functions of all of the banks. Second, it is assumed that the goal of banks is to increase their wealth by increasing the funds in their reserve accounts with the central bank and that they succeed in so doing. Figure E-1 in Appendix E shows the historical fact that banks have increased their wealth over time.

The initial condition is that an economy exists and a quantity of money, designated as "MO" in the analysis, is present in the active economy.

Banks obviously could not operate without the initial money being in the economy. If there were no money in the economy and the bank loaned $1000 for a year at 10% interest then the bank would need to be repaid $1100 at the end of a year but the additional $100 is not there. A noted analyst, faced with explaining this basic fact said some people would claim God put that initial money in the economy! However it was done, that initial money, MO, must be in the economy for banks to operate and for an analysis to proceed.

The analysis that is shown in Appendix E is of commercial bank operations only and from that analysis it is possible to show what role the central bank and federal government can and should play.

It is assumed also that a national debt exists and is used by the central bank in the management of the monetary system.

The federal government spends money into the economy, takes money out by taxes and by borrowing, thereby creating the national debt. Government spending is generally considered to be balanced by the sum of taxes collected plus funds borrowed equaling the amount spent.

There is, however, some spending which is not balanced nor does it appear on the balance sheet for the federal government except in an innocuous sounding footnote.

This government spending into the economy that increases money in the economy and is not balanced by either taxes or borrowing is seigniorage or the difference between the cost to produce a money object and the face value of the object.

For example, it costs the US Treasury 0.0959 dollars (2016) to mint a quarter of a dollar, that 0.0959 being spent into the economy to produce the coin and balanced by an equal amount taken from the economy by taxes and borrowing.

Thus, when the quarter is placed in the Treasury's account at the Federal Reserve and then spent a total of 0.2500 minus 0.0959 or 0.1541 will be added to the money in the economy. Noteworthy is the fact that this 0.1541 is money that is free of debt. It does not have to be repaid to a bank at interest. This type of money is called sovereign money.

The same process occurs with any monetary item created and spent by the federal government. Examples are the "greenbacks" spent by Lincoln to pay for the civil war and US Notes that were printed and spent from 1862 until Jan. 1971. Silver certificates were also sovereign money and they were printed and spent from 1878 until 1964.

Coins with which we are familiar have low seigniorage. Pennies and nickels have a negative seigniorage. Only dimes and quarters have positive seigniorage.

Half dollars are no longer minted and dollar coins never became popular for circulation. Both had significant positive seigniorage.

Paper currency carries a large seigniorage. The Treasury prints a one hundred dollar note for just $0.14, giving a seigniorage of $99.86 on each bill. The seigniorage of Federal Reserve notes does not accrue to the benefit of the people and the government. Commercial banks derive interest on the seigniorage of Federal Reserve notes when they make loans.

The other process by which money can be added to the economy is by the Federal Reserve's FOMC (Federal Open markets Committee) buying national debt. If debt is purchased from individuals or entities in the economy then the purchase price results in money being added to the economy. If the bonds are purchased from banks then the proceeds go into the bank reserve accounts, enabling the bank to loan more money but it does not add money directly to the economy.

The Fed's much discussed QE programs fell into this category; the multi T$ spent by the Fed went into banks reserves, not into the economy and therefore there was no direct danger of inflation from the process.

The analysis given in Appendix E only considers the total dollars placed into the economy and taken out of the economy by commercial bank loans. It does not consider money inserted by sovereign spending by the federal government nor of debt monetization by the Fed. The results of the analysis can be used, however, to identify the action needed by government fiscal policy and Fed monetary policy to mitigate against "booms and busts" in the economy. The analysis also shows the difficulty of "getting it right" to prevent crashes.

Two policy options for banks are examined in the analysis shown in Appendix E. One option is for the bank to make loans of the same amount each year. The second option is for the bank to make loans in a fashion that maintains a fixed amount of money in the economy. It can be noted that Fed policy is an extension of this later policy. The Fed goal is to increase the money supply at a nominal rate of 2 to 3% per year.

The analysis shows that both options are unstable if there is no support by federal government sovereign spending or Fed monetizing of the debt. The first option, constant loans each year, will deplete the money in the economy and transfer it into bank reserve accounts over a period of time, $y_x = L_f/i_r$, as shown in Appendix E. L_f is the ratio of the amount of money originally in the economy to the amount of the annual loans made by banks. The historical value of i_r is .074. Hence, if the loans are twice the amount of original money in the economy, the chaos point is reached in 6.8 years, about what Dimon told Warren.

Appendix E shows that the second option, maintaining a fixed amount of money in the economy, is also unstable. The quantity of money loaned by banks must increase exponentially to accomplish maintaining a fixed sum of money in the economy.

The expression for the annual loan amount derived in Appendix E is:

$$L(y) = L_o * (1 + i_r)^{y-1}$$

It is an exponential expression. An exponential is a function that increases at a rate equal to its value. In other words, the bigger it gets, the faster it increases. When the value is one then it will increase at a rate of one per year. When the value becomes 1000 then it will be increasing at a rate of 1000 per year. This, in fact, is the historical experience of the money supply as shown in Figure 5. The money supply since the early 1930s has risen exponentially at a rate of about 6.9% per year. The significant "bump" in the '40s is a reflection of the extraordinary monetary policies applied during the WWII years.

By lending out exactly what was collected the previous year, the amount of money in the economy remains constant. The crisis point is reached when the loan repayment exceeds the fixed amount of money in the economy or, as shown in Appendix E, when:

$$y_x = 32.3 * \log(M0/L_o) + 1 \text{ years}$$

Examples of the result are shown in the table in Appendix E.

The policy actions that the Fed and/or the federal government need to take to avoid the catastrophic effects of reaching a point where loan repayments exceed money in the economy is obvious. The Fed and/or the federal government must pump money into the economy to forestall reaching that point. The Fed can put money into the economy by buying debt and the federal government can add money by spending seigniorage and, more indirectly, by deficit spending which moves money in the economy from an idle state to a more active state.

The analysis is of a quasi-static scenario but it does predict the actual exponential build up of money in the economy. The real world case, however, is very dynamic. The value of M0 used in the analysis as a constant is not actually constant and will be a function of both government and Fed policy and time line of actions taken. Getting all of those actions correct in both magnitude and timing to avoid a crash is not a simple task and is made more difficult by the separation of monetary actions by the Fed and fiscal actions by the federal government.

Data is available showing the actions of the government and the Fed before and after the '09 crash. Figures 4 and Figure 6, above, shows the national debt which describes deficit spending and the Fed's holding of national debt which reflects their open market operations to put money in and take money out of the economy.

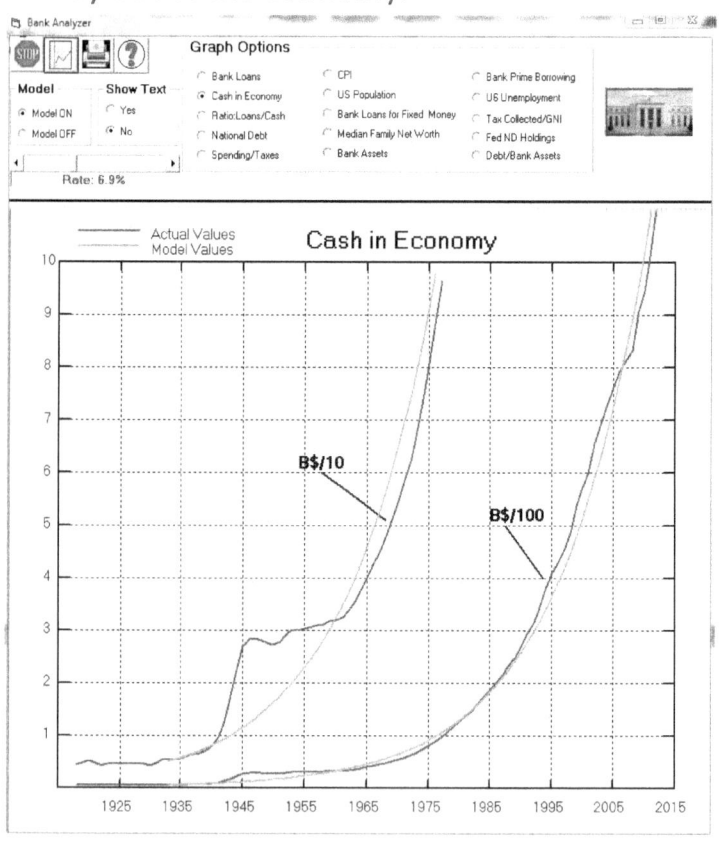

Figure 6: Money in the Economy

The dip in the holdings near '08 shows the Fed recognizing the heating up of the economy and removing money from the economy by selling debt. That action can be considered a key, or at minimum, one of the real causes for the crash. Immediately after the crash the Fed went on a buying spree to pump money back in the economy.

The national debt shows, by the year to year change, the deficit spending by the government. In figure 6, the slight downturn near 2000, is Bill Clinton's much discussed surplus years when tax revenue was greater than expenditures. At the time of the crash the debt was increasing very fast, meaning the deficits were large.

The magnitude of the effects of the '09 crash is startling. Figures 7 and 8 show the change in the assets of the twelve federal reserve banks and the reserve accounts of the commercial banks in the federal reserve system. Everyone knows the changes that occurred on "Main Street." The graphs show what happened on "Wall Street."

The twelve privately owned Fed regional banks experienced a tripling of their assets and the reserves of commercial banks (their actual wealth) increased seven fold. It was the fastest and largest transfer of wealth ever experienced in this nation. A crash can be very bad for average citizens but with programs such as TARP and QE banks can make out very well.

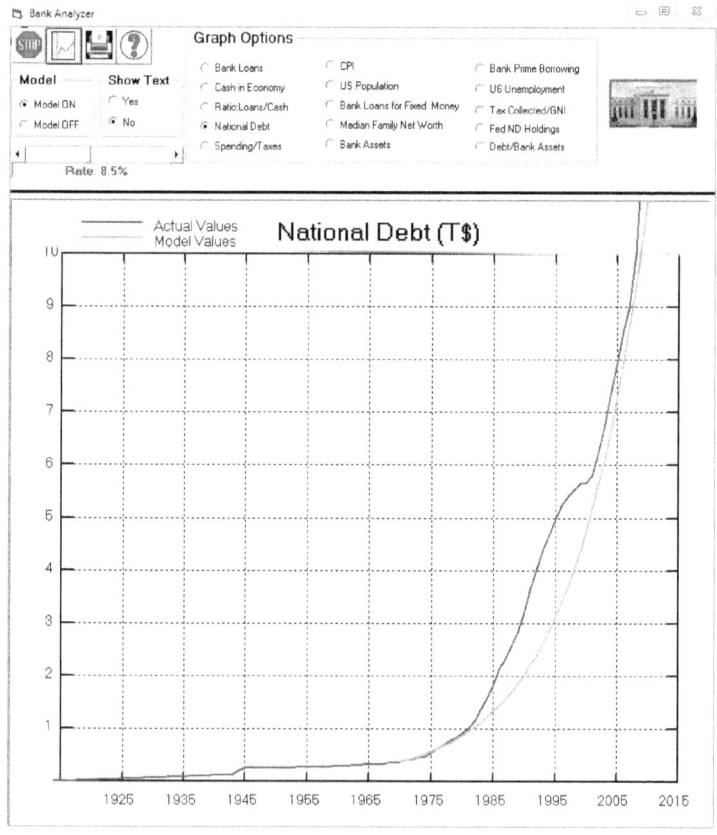

Figure 7: The National Debt

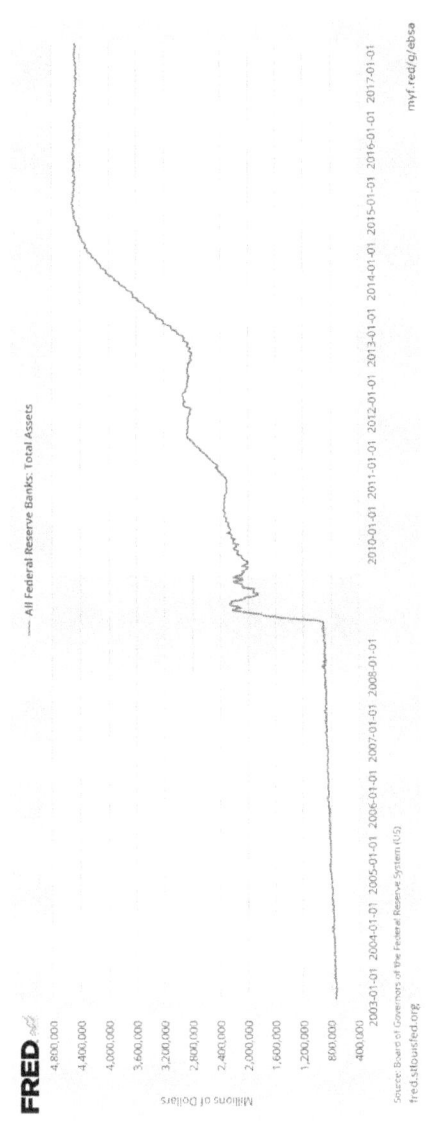

Figure 8: Federal Reserve Banks Total Assets

Figure 9: Bank Reserve Balances

The reserves of banks increased by a factor of 429, from 6.5B$ to 2.8T$, over the period from June of 2008 to Sept 2014. That is an average increase of 67% per year. Meanwhile the net worth of American households took a nose dive as shown previously in the figure 3. The median family lost $63,000 and, with over 100 million families in the USA, that is a loss of about 6.3T$. Meanwhile commercial bank reserves increased by about 2.8T$ and the assets of the twelve federal reserve banks increased by 3.6T$ for a total of about 6.4T$. It was an enormous transfer of wealth from American families to the banking system.

Perhaps we should have listened to Thomas Jefferson and Abraham Lincoln:

"If the American people ever allow private banks to control the issue of their currency, first by inflation, then by deflation, the banks...will deprive the people of all property until their children wake-up homeless on the continent their fathers conquered.... The issuing power should be taken from the banks and restored to the people, to whom it properly belongs."

– **Thomas Jefferson** in the debate over the Re-charter of the Bank Bill (1809)

"The Government should create, issue, and circulate all the currency and credits needed to satisfy the spending power of the Government and the buying power of consumers. By the adoption of these principles, the taxpayers will be saved immense sums of interest. Money will cease to be master and become the servant of humanity." **-Abraham Lincoln**

Chapter 7

Sovereign vs. Debt Money

Many discussions and proposals for modifying the existing banking and monetary system have been described and discussed in previous chapters. The truly big choice, however, is between the present system, often called "debt money", or using a system of sovereign spending to supply money to the economy. It is interesting to note that Dr. Ben Bernanke, in a posting on his blog, refers to this type of funding of government operations as using "money" as opposed to "debt." He also puts this type of funding in the same category as "helicopter money" as first described by Milton Friedman.

The minting of T$ coins as discussed above would have been a step in that direction but POTUS rejected the proposal probably because of pressure from the banking sector.

The difference between the two systems is

enormous in many dimensions. The power centers are different, the responsibilities for management of the economic system fall in different places and the benefits of the system accrue to different groups.

Changes of this magnitude are not easy to make. The groups that enjoy the benefits of the present system will not easily give up their powers.

The important thing is for the citizens of this nation to understand the present system, how it works and who benefits from it. They also need to understand how and to whom the benefits of a new system would accrue. They must also understand the shift in responsibilities that would occur and what would be expected from the parties who would have these new responsibilities.

Lastly, they would need to understand and know what would be expected from them with the new system. With all of this information under their collective belts the nation's citizens could exercise their power under our democracy and choose the system that is best for the nation.

There is a relevant side note. The discussions and proposals for a new monetary system have not gone unnoticed by parties who would suffer from these changes. The TPP had in it a requirement that would "lock in" the present western style banking and monetary systems in the countries of all signees. Obama, in supporting the TPP said that "...if we don't make the rules then China will..." China does use a different monetary system which is much closer to sovereign money than is ours at the present time.

Looking analytically at the two monetary systems, endogenous or debt money and sovereign money spending, it is immediately obvious that the endogenous system is more complex and many parts are obscured by the closed door operations of the Federal Reserve. A sovereign system also has its challenges and somewhat obscure parts but it is easier to understand and to analyze.

We must take the systems one at a time to develop an understanding of each. Starting with the existing endogenous system, we will first look at the intent of the approach and then the processes that underlies the system. In the following discussion "endogenous system" will be designated the ES.

Our current ES that was sold to Woodrow Wilson in 1913 was the third central bank approved for operation in the USA. It was sold as a system that would automatically regulate and sustain the proper amount of money in the economy for the economic conditions at any given time. It would differ in detail from the first two but would be "the lender of last resort" for banks facing runs.

Gold was money and gold certificates were printed to serve as circulating currency for the first twenty years of the Feds operation. These paper certificates were printed by the US Treasury Bureau of Engraving and Printing and given to the Federal Reserve for the cost of printing.

The monetary system has changed many times over the life time of the nation, usually because of a chaotic event. Bank panics in 1907 and 1929 are two examples. The '07 panic spawned the Federal Reserve and the '29 crash lead to removal of the gold standard by FDR. It is time for another overhaul of our monetary system and, hopefully, it can be done before, not after another chaotic event.

The political obstacles will be huge because the monetary system is the seat of power and privilege and those who now hold these powers will fight to maintain their privileges.

Our existing monetary system provides

wealth to banks that should accrue to the nation as a whole and to the citizens of the nation. How this happens is a complex issue but it involves the basic central bank system (the Fed) that we use.

Demonstrating it is an actual fact is very easy to do using some simple logic plus facts published by the Federal Reserve.

We need a Gedankenexperiment where we assume we have a 100% sovereign money spending government. That is, the government prints money and strikes coins and spends/issues them directly into the economy without borrowing.

We most also assume that after spending money the government must then redeem a portion of the spent money by way of taxation to prevent the accumulation of too much or an inflationary amount of money in the economy. We will assume also that bookkeeping is used to document the amount of spending and the amount of redemptions by taxation. In the bookkeeping we will assume the total spent minus the amount redeemed is equal to a national debt. The following table illustrates the results of this action by a government spending only sovereign money. The intriguing and obvious result is that the amount of money in the economy is equal to the accumulated national debt as stated by the bookkeeping.

Year	$ Spent	Tax $	$ in Economy	Debt
1	1000	-0-	1000	1000
2	1200	200	2000	2000
3	1400	200	3200	3200
4	1600	300	4500	4500
5	1800	400	5700	5700

Understanding how sovereign spending by a government would work, i.e., that the national debt would be equal to the total money in the economy, we can now look at the relationship of the national debt to features of our central bank system with money placed into the economy by bank loans rather than directly by government spending.

We find the answer by comparing the national debt to assets of commercial banks. The following graph, figure 10, using data published by the Fed, shows that relationship over the years from 1934 to 2015. The results are startling. Over those years the average ratio of the national debt to the assets of commercial banks is just under unity. It is suggested that the ratio is just under unity because of the limited spending of sovereign money by the government.

Banks, by making loans, sweep all money eventually out of the economy by way of interest collections. Since sovereign spending does not add to the debt the bank assets become slightly greater than the national debt.

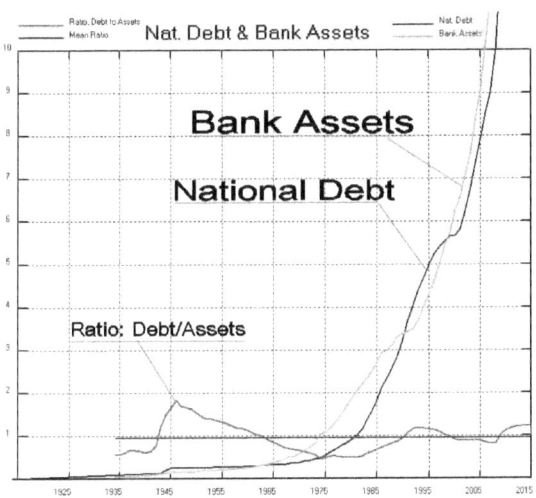

Figure 10: Ratio of Debt to Bank Assets

From this we can plainly see the difference between our endogenous money system with bank loans being the source of money in the economy (debt money) and a government which spends sovereign money directly into the economy. When the government spends directly into the economy then the money stays in the economy and can move freely in the economy until it is removed by taxes. The money moves freely for transactions in the economy and never accrues degradation by interest charges.

Now, with our present central bank model, government spending deficits become commercial bank assets instead of money moving freely in the economy. It is an astounding difference that is supported by simple logic and historical fact. We often hear "...the system is rigged..." This is the ultimate rigging; money that should be flowing freely in the economy with no interest derived by it becomes instead the wealth of commercial banks.

Over the past eight decades since the crash of '29 the government spending of sovereign monies has steadily decreased. Before the crash of '29 six types of paper currency were in use as listed below. Three of the six were sovereign money, US Notes, Gold and Silver Certificates. These are the six currencies used prior to the '29 crash:

United States Notes
Gold Certificates
National Bank Notes
Silver Certificates
Federal Reserve Bank Notes
Federal Reserve Notes

Three remained after FDR closed the banks and took the nation off the gold standard for domestic transactions. Two of the three sovereign currencies remained as follows:

United States Notes
Silver Certificates
Federal Reserve Notes

In Jan of 1970 the last sovereign currency, US Notes, was discontinued. Silver Certificates had been discontinued in the '60s. The only remaining paper currency was Federal Reserve Notes and the only sovereign money issued by the federal government was coins.

At present four types of coins are minted and

circulated; pennies, nickels, dimes and quarters. Pennies and nickels carry a negative seigniorage, costing more to mint than their face value. Only dimes and quarters carry a positive seigniorage, costing less to mint than their face value.

The reduction of sovereign spending by the government has benefited banks, giving them more control and greater benefits from the monetary system. It has also made the economy less efficient and reduced the benefits of the monetary system to the citizens of the nation.

A major portion of circulating money in the economy should be from sovereign spending by the government with credit money from banks supplying the sporadic needs of the economy. Our economy was more vibrant and prospered more when the government spent more sovereign money into the economy as was done in the war years of the 40s and continued into the 50s when the national economy was very vibrant.

A key contributor to that vibrancy was the US National Bank, the RFC, which could borrow directly from the US Treasury to support programs in the economy as detailed in Appendix I. China has copied the monetary and fiscal policies we used with such success in the 40s and 50s to produce their very vibrant economy. They have organized four banks, the four largest banks in the world, patterned after the RFC we used from the 30s until it was closed by Eisenhower in the late 50s.

We need the benefits of a national bank again to enable spending sovereign monies into the economy, utilizing idle resources to repair our infrastructure, provide healthcare and other programs that would benefit the economy and all citizens of the nation.

#

Chapter 8

The misunderstanding of the function of taxes in our monetary system is very harmful to our political system for two basic reasons. First, it detracts from discussions and action related to the actual function of taxes plus it constrains government actions that are needed and worthwhile.

The falsehood that taxes are needed to "pay" for government operations permeates our political system. Many in politics are surely aware of this falsehood but I have never heard it mentioned by anyone in active political life.

It is obvious that the government cannot extract taxes to operate the government before spending money into the economy. The government must first create the money and spend it into the economy before it can be redeemed for taxes. Taxes have a number of functions but paying for government operations is not one of them.

Ronald Regan made the catch phrase "tax and spend" a household word for describing liberals. It was, however, an erroneous statement. The government cannot "tax and spend." It is impossible. The cycle must be and is "spend and tax."

Spending and taxing is not a new idea. The Virginia colonial government was totally aware of this fact in March 1760 when they passed the paper money act, (see Appendix B) creating money, and in the same legislation, arranging to place tax liabilities on the public to take back a portion of the money and, in their words, "... to preserve the credit of the paper currency..." The legislation required that redeemed certificates were "... to be burnt and destroyed." Taxes do give value to paper currency but they are not used to pay for government operations. The notion that taxes are needed to pay for government expenses is a figment of the imagination of bookkeepers but it is totally divorced from reality.

In January 1946, in the periodical "American Affairs", Beardsley Ruml, Chairman of the Federal Reserve Bank of New York at that time, published an article (see Appendix A) entitled " TAXES FOR

REVENUE ARE OBSOLETE" in which he explains why taxes do not pay for government operations. As explained in the paper, it started in 1933 when, under FDR, fiat currency was introduced and gold money and gold certificates were all redeemed for the new currency. Noteworthy is the fact the new currency spent by the government was not obtained by taxing. It was printed and spent into the economy to buy gold and gold certificates.

The actual function of taxes is to maintain price stability (i.e. prevent inflation) and secondly, it enables the government to move money around in the economy by taxing "A" and spending to "B." Tax policy has obviously been one factor in the movement of wealth from the middle class to the 1% over the past few decades.

Additionally, taxes can be a very efficient economic tool. We saw that feature used very sparingly in recent years with the FICA tax holidays which put money in the pockets of consumers who represent the major portion of our economy. It was used very sparingly because of the book keeping fairy tale that the FICA/SS trust fund "pays" social security to seniors, the same fairy tale as the one that taxes pay for government operations.

Book keepers can put numbers in columns and add and subtract them but their actions have zero effect on the realities of money. The reality is that all legal money is created by the US Treasury in their Bureau of Engraving and Printing (BEP) and their mints where coins are struck. The fiscal assets of the government are infinite. The only real limits on government spending is the availability of real resources to buy and general price stability in the economy.

The IRS, the government agency charged with responsibility for "collecting" taxes is well known by all adult Americans. The agency, without doubt, is so onerous some would think they should have a fourth letter in their name so they could join the ranks of our other 4-letter words.

That said, some very interesting facts can be gleaned by looking at the cost of operating the IRS and the quantity of taxes they collect. Looking at the year 2014, the IRS budget was 11.9B$ and collections were 2.59T$. That sounds like a pretty good investment but, if the 11.9B$ spent on operating the IRS were allocated to the BEP (Bureau of Engraving and Printing), they could have printed 11.9T$ in $100 bills, each bill costing just under ten cents to print[9].

And paper currency is the expensive kind of money. The money created by keyboard clicks and by computer programs as used to pay the principal and interest on the national debt and social security benefits is even cheaper to create.

All monies taken by the federal government are taxes. It may be called a fee or a tariff but it is still just action to remove money from the economy. Some of the processes are necessary and very useful. Fees for government service, although they do not "pay" for the service, they do discourage overuse of a service.

The destruction of money by taxes and fees is easy to understand when you consider the difference between taking money, safeguarding it, maintaining accountability and transporting it vs. just destroying it and recreating it at a different location. If gold were still money this simplification of the process could not be done. Fiat money enabled these transactions to be done in a much easier way. Fiat money is easier to destroy and then recreate

---

[9] The current cost of printing a $100 bill is slightly more than 14 cents

elsewhere than to store and transport it. This feature of fiat money makes it free and plentiful to the federal government as explained by Beardsley Ruml in appendix A.

I have heard the reality of taxes being a way to destroy money can be demonstrated by paying your taxes at an IRS office. If you pay your tax bill with cash at an IRS office they will take your cash and shred it. They will not take coins because they cannot, under law, destroy coins. Amazingly, the process is identical to that used in 1760 by the Virginia Colony as described in appendix B.

The different treatment of coins and paper currency brings up another fact concerning the monetary system. The US currently has two separate and distinct monetary systems in operation, coins and paper notes, and they work together, for the most part, in a seamless fashion. Coins are minted by US mints and placed in the governments account at face value regardless of the cost of minting the coins. The seigniorage for pennies and nickels is negative; it costs more to mint them than their face value. The other coins have positive seigniorage; in 2010 a quarter was minted for just 11 cents and dollar coins are for just 18 cents.

Paper notes, on the other hand, are printed by the US Treasure's Bureau of Engraving and Printing (BEP) and then sold to the Federal Reserve for the cost of printing. A $100 bill costs about 15 cents to print and it is printed with great sophistication to foil counterfeiters.

How taxes are imposed on taxpayers is an ongoing political issue. Most of the discussion, ignoring the arguments concerning deductions, centers on "tax brackets" and the rates charged in each bracket. It is generally agreed by all that higher incomes should be taxed at a higher rate than lower incomes or progressive taxation is the proper way to set up tax policy. A problem arises when "bracket creep" comes into play when a small increase can land the taxpayer in a higher bracket or, by working deductions, a taxpayer may be able to slip down into a lower bracket.

Current technology provides a way around this issue. A dollar wide bracket tax system can be easily imposed as described in technical detail in appendix G. The dollar wide bracket system can be established by imposing three or more income level, tax rate points. From these points a smooth, continuous tax rate can be defined where a person earning $66,500.00 would pay a slightly lower tax rate than a person earning $66,501.00.

A key conceptual difference in the dollar wide tax bracket scheme is that a person earning $200,000.00 per year will pay the same rate on the first $20,000.00 of his income as a person who earns only $20,000.00 per year. He will, however, pay a higher rate on the remaining $180,000.00 of income. This conceptual difference enables the development of a continuous dollar wide tax bracket process.

A computer program is available that enables the user to interactively set up trial points and evaluate tax collection versus total national income using a math model of income distribution. The model is based on data from the Census Bureau for 2016.

The model and data available on income distribution is a function described as total dollars earned vs. level of income. The value of this function is very high a lower levels of income, peaking in the region of $40,000 to $60,000 because of the large number of people with earnings in these levels. The value of the function decreases rapidly in the $150,000 to $200,000 region with fewer and fewer earners in those regions. The data from the government is very course, reported in very wide brackets but the amount of money involved is large because of the width of the reported brackets. This makes accurate modeling difficult but not inaccurate because for almost any tax policy the rate at some high level of income will be constant for all income levels in excess of some amount. For this reason the process used in the program with an analytical model can be useful in designing a dollar wide tax system.

It can be said that a dollar wide tax bracket system would be well received by everyone. It is rational and fair. Additionally, it would be a natural tool and very useful if and when an AI system is created to replace the Fed's FOMC as discussed in Chapter 12, "The Promise of New Technologies."

Chapter 9

Capitalism, Socialism and Religions

The substantial difference between capitalism and socialism is in the concept of money, how it is used, who creates it and how national governments finance programs. Capitalism is not a designed ideology. The origin is much debated and sometimes traced back in time to early man engaging in trade with neighbors. This view is used to label capitalism as a natural behavior pattern of man. The origin depends on how the ideology is defined. Most would agree, however, that capitalism was in full display as the industrial revolution matured in the early eightieth century.

Socialism is more of a designed system, springing from the works of Karl Marx. Socialists believe that governments, being an organization of the citizens on a nation, should supply the services and universal needs of the people that cannot or are not supplied by the "market place" at an affordable price.

If we view "capitalists" and "socialists" as being the top tier labels, we can find many shades inside each grouping. Conservatives support the capitalist agenda even when they are clearly not capitalists. The conservative, "take care of yourself" mantra, drives them to support the capitalist agenda of small government and having free enterprise supply all the needs of people.

Socialism has probably spawned the most sub labels. In the array from this camp we find communism at one extreme and neoliberals at the other end. The neoliberals, being so close to the capitalists while supporting a liberal social agenda, are even seen as being in another place. Bill Clinton described it as being the "third way."

In this era, the greatest evolutionary action is definitely in the socialist arena. Capitalism has become old fashioned, succumbing to the "stuck in the mud" syndrome. On the socialist side we see democratic socialism, practiced by many small nations in Europe, on full display by the Bernie Sanders campaign in 2016.

The current greatest and most significant maturing socialist ideology is occurring in China along with the "BRIC" nations (Brazil, Russia, India, China) allied together with China. In the USA, the effort to pass the Transpacific Partnership agreement (TPP) was an obvious effort to drive a wedge between the western style capitalism practiced in the USA and their Pacific partners and China. President Obama, defending the TTP, declared, "If we don't make the rules, China will."

There is a third force at play in the monetary wars in addition to the BRICs and western capitalism. Islamic banking[10] is prevalent in the Islamic communities and nations around the world. The following material, taken from the referenced footnote, describes the basic difference between Islamic and western style banking. The difference is between interest, or riba, charged by western banks and the prohibition of riba by the Qur'an.

---

[10] http://www.islamic-banking.com/what_is_ibanking.aspx

"Commercial Banks in Muslim Lands

Western commercial banks date from about two and a quarter centuries ago, when the western world was dispensing with moral and ethical considerations in economics. When the Muslim world came into contact with the west, Muslims had two choices:

a) To accept commercial banking, arguing that the interest charged by them did not contain the element of riba prohibited in the Qur'an; or,

b) To accept that interest charged was riba and try to develop an alternative system of banking.

But ancient Muslim institutions, such as the Shari'ah courts, had been made ineffective by the colonial powers. Muslims had no alternative but to work with the colonial institutions, including commercial banking.

Nevertheless, during the 19th century, several religious scholars argued that the term riba referred to loans for consumption, which people found it difficult to repay, and not to commercial banking loans, where the debtor can repay from the profits.

But the Qur'an makes no distinction between loans for consumption and loans for productive purposes. So their views were rejected. As a consequence, modern commercial banking did not make much headway in Muslim countries and to this day the presents of the conventional framework still dominates the national financial system."

The political and military stand offs between the Islamic nations in the mid east and the US has been primarily about resources and the US drive to maintain hegemony in the region. The differences in banking and the interest/riba issue is also of great importance in the geopolitical struggle between the west and the Islamic countries. Unfortunately, the issue is basically never voiced by any in the US political arena nor is it ever brought to public attention by our media. It is a subject that can be discussed rationally and logically. The underlying problem is that what is at stake for western banking. Western banking is based totally on interest, not only to make profits but also as a tool to manage economies. Conceptually the two systems are separated by a huge rift. Each party, western banking and Islamic law, has a lot at stake in the struggle. The citizens of the western world and the Islamic world both deserve to know and understand the dimension of the rift and what it means.

All of us need to know and appreciate the three way geopolitical struggle ongoing for domination of the way we create, use and disperse monies into our economies and, hopefully, work to find an accommodation to reduce the strife between the three major systems currently in use.

Chapter 10

A National Savings Bank

A National Savings Bank (NSB) where all citizens could hold accounts should be chartered. It would serve many purposes including those performed through the RFC during the 30s, 40s and 50s. It would enable reducing, and over time, retiring the national debt. Such a bank will be necessary if the national debt is to be retired.

The national debt now provides a place for entities with large idle money holdings, such as retirement accounts, to safely place their funds. The FDIC only covers $250,000 in deposits at commercial banks whereas treasury bonds are totally safe in any amount.

A National Savings Bank would also serve the same function as the national debt with respect to removal of money from the active economy. The debt, as a safe savings place for idle funds, is currently limited by the amount of deficit spending authorized by congress.

A National Savings Bank, open to all citizens in any amounts, would most probably attract greater deposits than the current national debt. The Post Offices could serve as depositories of savings. This has happened before. It is not new. Postal savings was used and legal under a law signed by President Taft and the postal savings system operated from January 1, 1911 until July 1, 1967. It was a total success but, as you can imagine, banks did not like it. Postal savings needs to be brought back again and its power to replace the national debt needs to be understood and recognized.

A National Savings Bank could serve many purposes. It is basically what is proposed by Ellen Brown and extensively described in her books. It would bring fundamental changes to our monetary system and how our government deals with money. The Treasury could establish their account with the NSB and pay all government obligations through that account. Currently the Treasury has an account with the Fed.

The Treasury could also make loans to itself

for long term programs such as infrastructure. This would be equivalent to present day deficit spending but with the NSB the loan interest would be essentially zero because any interest paid would be returned to the government. Being able to borrow from the NSB, the Treasury would not have to sell any more Treasury bonds and hence, over a period of 30 years, the national debt would be retired. This process, in effect, would convert the present national debt into assets of the new NSB.

As noted above, the idea of an NSB has been extensively analyzed and described by Ellen Brown in her book "Public Bank Solution." Additionally the establishment of an NSB has a president in the establishment in 1932 of the Reconstruction Finance Corporation or RFC.

The RFC operated from 1932 until 1957. The RFC was funded by the federal government, a significantly different approach from an NSB. The assets of the NSB would come from deposits made by all citizens and the entities that currently use the national debt as a savings account.

With the Treasury spending account transferred from the Fed to the NSB, the NSB would also enjoy the assets of the Treasury deposits including all sovereign money such as coins, US Notes and silver certificates. These sovereign currencies are not presently being created by the Treasury but could and should be used again. Silver certificates were discontinued during LBJ's term and US Notes were discontinued in Jan 1971.

The RFC was a bank, a national bank. At the height of its activities, it was probably the largest bank in the world. The history of the RFC is documented extensively on the Internet. One very complete history is available on the Internet[11] and is reprinted in an edited form in Appendix I. As described in this history, much of the great "war time economy" can be attributed to off budget spending through the RFC into the economy.

The US closed the RFC in 1957. The remnants that remained after closing the RFC were Fannie Mae, the Small Business Administration and the Import/Export Bank which were created by the RFC. The concept and economic effectiveness of the RFC did not go unnoticed, however. At the present time China has essentially duplicated and enhanced the

---

11   https://eh.net/encyclopedia/reconstruction-finance-corporation/

RFC concept in its organization of nationalized banks which are now the four largest banks in the world as shown in the following table:

Rank	Bank Name	Assets(US B$)
1	Industrial and Commercial Bank of China	3,475.34
2	China Construction Bank Corporation	3,018.40
3	Agricultural Bank of China	2,817.74
4	Bank of China	2,613.12

China's rapid economic growth can be attributed to them copying the method the USA had proven to be very effective for generating economic growth.

Also, the economic stagnation in the USA can be blamed on the refusal of our congress and government generally to not follow methods we had proven to be effective. Establishing a National Savings Bank would be a good first step in using methods we have proven to be effective and thereby enhance our economy to catch up with the new evolving economies such as China.

Chapter 11

The Wisdom of Thomas Jefferson

Thomas Jefferson was the third president of the USA, serving from 1801 to 1809. He was a staunch opponent of the national bank proposed by Alexandria Hamilton in the early 1790s. The bank had been created in 1791 during the term of President George Washington and it was given a twenty year charter. Twenty percent of the bank was owned by the government and eighty percent by private investors.

Jefferson, before the end of his second term in office, posed arguments against extending the bank's charter past its end date in 1811. One argument given by Jefferson was as follows:

"If the American people ever allow private banks to control the issue of their currency, first by inflation, then by deflation, the banks…will deprive the people of all property until their children wake-up homeless on the continent their fathers conquered…. The issuing power should be taken from the banks and restored to the people, to whom it properly belongs."
– **Thomas Jefferson** *in the debate over the Recharter of the Bank Bill (1809)*

The environmental factors of that era, social, economic, demographic and technological, were very different then from now. It is difficult to relate their detailed arguments in that era to our times but Jefferson's understanding of banks and what they do, is as current as the crash in 1929 and eighty years later, in 2009.

In the USA we have experienced the booms with inflation and the "too-little-money" syndrome of deflation following booms that burst when the economy has less money in circulation than loan repayments demand.

It happened during the great depression of the '30s and it happened again in the 2008 downturn. The visible indicators of the situation are copious signs of property for sale, real estate, homes, cars and many other items. People are forced to sell their property to obtain cash money and they are forced to sell at ever lower prices.

There is a whispered name for this situation among those benefited by it. It is a "liquidation phase" where people are forced to sell property because of the sacristy of money imposed by the monetary system. This name was attached to the bust after a boom by **Andrew Mellon as quoted in "Memoirs", Herbert Hoover, (1952). Melon is quoted as saying: "Liquidate labor, liquidate stocks, liquidate the farmers, liquidate real estate.... It will purge the rottenness out of the system."**

Both property and labor are liquidated when too little money is in the economy. Workers must liquidate their labor by working for ever lower wages. The groups who benefit from this situation are obvious. Those with saved money can purchase property at lower prices and employers can hire workers at lower wages.

Thomas Jefferson, over two hundred years ago, was fully aware of this cycle created by banks. The charter of Alexandria Hamilton's bank was not extended in 1811; Jefferson won that round. Five years later the proponents for chartering a national bank were back and in 1816 the Second US Bank was chartered for twenty years. Twenty years later Andrew Jackson defeated Nicolas Biddle and Henry Clay among others to block extending the second bank's charter.

Then, as we know, on the day before Christmas eve in 1913, Woodrow Wilson signed the Federal Reserve Act, creating a national bank again with a twenty year charter. We are still living with the Fed that manages and controls our economic system giving us a cycle of booms and busts, each cycle transferring wealth to banks and the more affluent from those with less monetary resources just as Jefferson stated.

Senator Elizabeth Warren, in her book "A Fighting Chance", quotes Jami Dimon on page 177 as saying: "...a financial crisis every five to seven years was inevitable..." She follows that statement with her own: "He was wrong."

I would suggest Thomas Jefferson and Jami Dimon understood banking much better that Elizabeth Warren. We need systemic changes in our monetary system to avoid the chaos seen in the system by Thomas Jefferson and fully understood by Dimon. Regulations as proposed by Senator Warren will not accomplish the job. Real and significant changes are needed in the monetary system in recognition of the wisdom of Thomas Jefferson.

Chapter 12

The Rigged System

We hear it often. The system is rigged! Many believe it. Some know it and many feel it. If we mean by "rigging" that some get more out of the system than others because of how the system is set up and run then, yes, the system is rigged.

There is one big "rig" that affects all of us and one that oppresses a nominal one in ten to one in twenty working adults in the nation.

The big rig is our monetary system that systematically shifts government deficit spending into assets of commercial banks instead of allowing the deficit spending to remain in the economy, interest free, for use by the economy. If the government were to spend sovereign money directly into the economy then the money could circulate interest free causing the federal "debt" to be identical to the interest free money circulating in the economy.

Figure 10, page 91 shows the historical fact that bank assets very closely follow the national debt. It shows something else too; a very important demonstration of the economic results of sovereign spending by the government.

During the war years the debt exceeded bank assets by a large margin, peaking in 1946 at a ratio of 1.83. It was a time, too, of a very vibrant economy enabled by the copious spending of sovereign money using the RFC, a US national bank chartered under Hoover in 1932, used extensively by the FDR administrations in the 30s and during the war years. The RFC was closed during the Eisenhower administration in the late 50s.

The second "rig" in the system is more insidious. There is even a well known notion firmly engrained in many that actually denies the reality of the issue. We have all heard the mantra, "Work hard, learn, stick with it and you will be OK" or some version thereof. It is engrained into us so deeply that it could and often is called "The American Way."

It is, however, a fable for 5 to 10% of the working population who will be denied jobs because of an erroneous assumption. The error is based on the Philipp's Curve, Figure 11, which purports to show that runaway inflation would result from very low unemployment and that "acceptable" inflation will be experienced when unemployment is held at or near 4.5 to 5.5%.

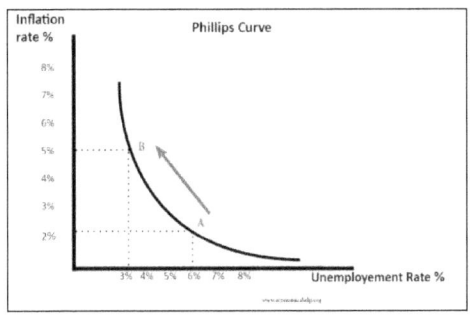

Figure 11: Phillips Curve

Unfortunately, with about 156 million in the workforce, 5.5% is 8.6 million souls who are denied jobs by the system. The official unemployment rate (U3) is 4.3% and the broadest measure of unemployment, U6, is 8.4% in 2017. Using the 156 million workforce number this is 6.7 million not working and looking for work and a total of 13.1 million with no jobs including those who have stopped looking. It is a lot of people and a monstrous waste of human resources all based on the fallacious assumption that some must be unemployed in order to hold inflation in check.

A recent study ("Who is out of the Labor Force?", August 2017) by The Hamilton Project at the Brookings Institute found that the actual number of working age adults not in the labor force to be about twenty four (24) million in 2016. This is a huge number, close to one in five working age adults. The study report is worth reading. It describes the demographics of the population that is out of the work force and seeks an understanding of why it has happened. The study finds recent events in the economic system such as the recession starting on '09, to be a major driver for the large cadre of persons who are no longer in the work force.

There is, I believe, a much simpler explanation. Our basic economic system, demanding a significant cadre of workers to be unemployed at any one time, has, over time, evolved a large group of people who have just given up on being employed and being a part of the labor force. I believe also that the partial employment mandate is a significant cause for the high incarceration rate in this nation. Crime is one option for the unemployed to access resources for sustaining a livelihood.

The Phillips Curve which is used to justify our economic policy of partial employment, was developed from thirty-five (35) data points taken between 1913 and 1948. Alban W. H. Phillips (1914–1975), a New Zealand economist, developed the curve from those data points and suggested an inverse relationship between the value of unemployment and inflation which is now used by the Federal Reserve in management of our economy.

The theory has been thoroughly debunked but our nation's economy is still managed on the bases of the Phillips Curve theory. In mid June, 2017, the Fed hiked prime interest rates based on the reported values of unemployment (U3: 4.3%, U6: 8.4%), tightening the money supply to slow the economy and impede increases in employment.

The fact that our economy is operated and managed in this way, based on a debunked theory, presents serious questions on both moral and economic grounds. The underlying purpose of tightening the money supply and slowing the economy is to maintain an unemployed pool of workers to put downward pressure on wages by having a labor supply that exceeds demand.

Looking first at the moral issues that surround this economic policy, the concept of "a job," what it is and what it does, must be investigated. A job is currently framed in the public eye as a means to take care of one's self and one's dependants. In actual, observable fact, a job is essential diametrically the opposite of that. A job is really a license to help others. Whether the job is making hamburgers and fries for people to eat at a McDonald's or working on an assembly line to build SUVs for people to transport themselves, you are helping others when you work at your job. A strong corollary to this observation is that a "job" that does not result in helping others is not a legitimate job.

Framing a job in these terms allows us to understand the moral issues associated with forcing a pool of workers to be without work. If they do not have a job then they do not have a license to help others.

The options for those who are denied jobs are limited. Some may receive unemployment which is, using this framing for jobs, the government paying people to not help others. The morality of this action should be questioned. The acceptable moral action would be for the government to pay people to help others.

We know the unemployment pooling falls heavily on young intercity black youths. Chicago is an example of a city hard hit by unemployment[12] with nearly half of young black adults not having a job. Without a job and a license to help others they often turn, unfortunately, to crime, hurting others rather than helping others which they would do if they had a job.

The management policy for our economy should not be based on debunked theories such as the Phillip's Curve, and carried out with amoral consequences. There is general agreement among many economists that current policy can and should be replaced by a 100% employment policy, the federal government serving as an employer of last resort. This new policy is called the job guarantee program or "JG."

There is and has been a healthy debate ongoing regarding the specifics of such a policy change and the advantages and disadvantages of such a

---

[12]   http://www.chicagotribune.com/ct-youth-unemployment-urban-league-0126-biz-20160124-story.html

change. The central support for a JG[13] policy is at the University of Missouri-Kansas City's school of economics, home of the economics school of thought called Modern Money Theory[14] (MMT). Two of the leading voices for MMT are Dr. Stephaney Kelton and Dr. William Black. Both were tapped as economic advisors for the Bernie Sanders campaign in 2016.

These polices proposed by MMT at UMKC and numerous other schools of economics around the country have not yet reached the political table. History tells us, however, that any subject broadly endorsed by the economic community will eventually be placed on the political table. If the JG becomes a reality then one of the very significant "rigging" of the system will be defeated.

The moral aspect of the policy change to 100% employment using the JG is persuasive but economists also see and support the JG for basic

---

13

http://www.kansascity.com/news/business/article68304027.html

[14] http://neweconomicperspectives.org/

economic reasons[15]; that it will help build a more vibrant economy that will help everyone.

There are two very important points in the argument for a JG. First, it will fulfill the need to prevent run away wage levels. The current policy relies on supply being greater than demand to hold down wages; preventing what is called "wage inflation." The JG will maintain a fixed price for minimum wages with the time tested technique of a supplier offering to either buy or sell a commodity at the same price. The US employed this technique for many years to control the price of gold, being willing to either buy or sell it at the same price. The JG will establish a buy/sell policy at the JG wage level which will become the de facto minimum wage. Unemployment payments, a minimum wage and many welfare programs would be discarded with a JG program.

The economic impact from initiation of a JG program would be very significant. In the beginning the cadre of JG workers would be large, employing everyone who wished to work and had no job. The

---

15   http://neweconomicperspectives.org/2012/03/mmp-blog-43-job-guarantee-basics-design-and-advantages.html

influx of money into the economy from the JG pay-roll would greatly increase demand for goods and services, leading to greater need for workers in the private sector which would drain off JG workers by way of the needs of the private sector. In this manner, a JG would result in great benefits to both the labor force and also to private industry, ensuring a significant boost in GDP.

Chapter 13

The Promise of New Technologies

Computers and communications technologies over the past two decades have changed our lives. We, as a society, are adapting to these changes and evolving into a very different world. The young in today's world cannot imagine a world without "cells" and I, at my age, remember being awestruck when the first electric light was installed in our home and again when a crank telephone was mounted on the wall and connected to a party line.

These new communication technologies make news close to instantaneous and widely distributed on the Internet and by person to person and person to groups via social media. We can capture these assets to greatly improve our monetary system and national fiscal operations.

It is now possible, using these new computing and communication tools, to design a monetary/fiscal system that would be free of the boom/bust cycles that have haunted us for centuries, provide a stable currency and full employment for all willing workers.

These new technologies provide tools for operation of a monetary system undreamed of even in 1971 when the last significant modification to the system was made by Nixon, removing the US from the international gold standard.

These technologies and the rapidly developing field of Artificial Intelligence (AI) can be captured to greatly improve our monetary system and national fiscal operations.

Many people saw the capability of AI when IBM's Watson[16] performed on the Jeopardy game show. Watson, with his memory holding the books from the Library of Congress, handily defeated his human opponents. More recently Watson has been used in finding treatment options for cancer patients using the genetic alterations of the patient and the stored historical records of treatment re-

---

[16] Watson is a computer system capable of answering spoken questions. The computer was named after IBM's first CEO, Thomas J. Watson.

sults. An edge Watson has over mere humans is his ability to ingest the nominal eight thousand (8,000) new papers published each day on cancer treatments.

AI is a bourgeoning technology giving us the potential of driverless cars, humanoid robots and countless other applications that will transform our very lives.

It can also transform the operation of our monetary system. The Federal Open Markets Committee (FOMC) is the operational group that manages our money supple and our economy. Their goal is to adhere to the dual mandate, imposed on the Federal Reserve by the Congress, which is to maintain price stability and full employment. Full employment is defined as an unemployment rate between 5.2 and 5.5% and price stability is defined as an inflation rate of 2% per year.

The tools used by the FOMC are buying and selling the national debt and setting the interest rate that banks charge each other for overnight loans; also referred to as the federal funds rate.

The committee is chaired by the chairperson of the Fed, currently Janet Yellen, and has eight scheduled meetings each year. The other members of the committee are the Board of Governors plus selected presidents of Federal Reserve regional banks with the president of the New York Fed having a permanent ex officio seat.

Each of the twelve regional banks compile reports on the economic status of the region they serve for each meeting of the FOMC. The members of the committee apparently study these reports and reach conclusions on open market operations (buying/selling of national debt) and any needed adjustments to the Federal Funds Rate.

A control systems engineer looking at the functional relationship between the FOMC, the money supply, employment and price stability would immediately relate the process to a classic control system as shown in figure 12. The reference input is the Fed's dual mandate, the feedback is the reports furnished by the regional banks and the FOMC is the sum point, comparing the mandate with the reports. The forward process is the open market policy and Federal Funds rate imposed by the committee. The controlled output is then the economy generally and money supply, prices and employment.

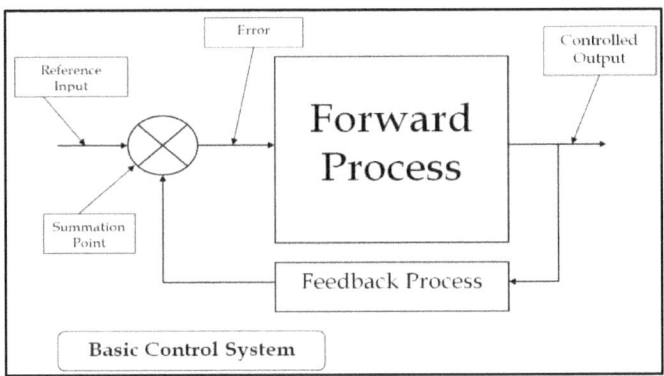

Figure 12: Basic Control System

Feedback systems or servo controls use a very old technology. It has been applied for many years to electro-mechanical systems and more recently to electronic systems. The control laws state that any system with only positive feedback will be unstable and a system with negative feedback will also be unstable unless the gain and time constants in the system are designed correctly to enable stability.

Natural processes we see in nature confirm these laws as natural laws. A noteworthy example is what is called species diversification. Archeologists have confirmed many cycles of increasing diversity, a peaking followed by a decline in bio-diversity. The bio-diversity system is driven by positive feedback and it oscillates between some natural minimum and maximum limits. A controls engineer would describe it as "banging against the stops." When a particular specie becomes extinct then the specie or species depending on it will also disappear.

William Machesney Martin, who served as Chairman of the Federal Reserve from 1951 through 1970, recognized the need for negative feedback in the monetary system when he said in a speech:

"If we fail to apply the brakes sufficiently and in time, of course, wc shall go over the cliff. If businessmen, bankers, your contemporaries in the business and financial world, stay on the sidelines, concerned only with making profits, letting the Government bear all of the responsibility and the burden of guidance of the economy, we shall surely fail. ... In the field of monetary and credit policy, precautionary action to prevent inflationary excesses is bound to have some onerous effects--if it did not it would be ineffective and futile. Those who have the task of making such policy do not expect you to applaud. The Federal Reserve, as one writer put it, after the recent increase in the discount rate, is in the position of the chaperone who has ordered the

punch bowl removed just when the party was really warming up."

He clearly understood the need for negative feedback to maintain stability of the economic system. He also understood another fundamental factor for achieving stability when he said, "...to apply the brakes sufficiently and in time." A control systems engineer would express the same need but in terms of gain and bandwidth.

The basic elements in the block diagram shown in Figure 12 can be related to functions and processes in the existing Federal Reserve System.

The summation point is the FOMC's policy decision on actions to be taken. The FOMC meets nominally eight times each year. The forward process is overnight interest rates and open market operations where the FOMC sets policy for buying and selling the national debt. The error is the difference between the Fed's mandated dual responsibility for employment and price stability and the condition of the economy as reported from the twelve regional Federal Reserve Banks.

Timing, just as Martin knew in 1951, is critically important. Loop gain, as it is called by control engineers, is also critically important. Gain is represented by the ratio of output divided by input or the feedback process output divided by the error.

In electro-mechanical systems the characteristics of all the elements can be defined with great accuracy and the control loop can be analyzed with precision for stability and accuracy. In the Federal Reserve System that level of exactness cannot be duplicated but significant observations can be made regarding the relative strengths and weaknesses in the existing system as they relate to the stability and accuracy of the system. An AI system, acting as the summation or error detecting point, could utilize both historical data on actions taken and results achieved plus use near real time data as available over communication lines.

Our recent experience following the '09 crash has shown the "Forward Process" in the loop to be ineffective, with a gain close to zero. The overnight interest rate was moved to almost zero and bank reserves became very large but the output, employment and prices, were not significantly affected. This was noted in the media by the observation that Wall Street was bailed out but Main Street had to suffer.

The "Feedback Process" would get an up check for quality but the lag/time constant of the data plus the sample rate controlled by the eight meetings per year make the system slow, and in control language, can introduce too much phase shift which can lead to instability.

The most difficult element in the system to analyze is the deliberations of the FOMC and their determination of the magnitude of the error. While they should be focused on their mandate, they are surely influenced by political realities plus their own subjective beliefs about the economy and the existing dynamics in the economy.

Another factor in the conundrum is the fact that things are happening faster in our economy because of the technologies of communications and computers. These improvements in technology have also assisted the Federal Reserve System by improving the quality, quantity and promptness of the data they gather through the twelve regional banks. One can only postulate that perhaps these technologies have had a more profound effect on the economy than they have had on the Federal Reserve.

One additional technical feature of the Federal Reserve viewed as a control system is the nature of the feedback and the type of control system the feedback represents.

In control system theory there are three major types; Type 0, Type 1 and Type 2. The Type 0 is also called a regulator. It has no integrator in the loop and requires an error to maintain the output. The Fed falls into this category.

A Type 1 has one integrator in the loop and is called a servo system. Under steady state conditions it provides a fixed output with zero error. A Type 2, with two integrators, provides a fixed rate of change of the output with zero error.

An insight into the types of control systems is useful in evaluating the differences between the present system and what can be done using modern communications and AI technology.

The feasibility of replacing the FOMC with an AI system such as IBM's Watson is very close to being a "no brainer." An AI system to perform the functions of the FOMC would probably be simpler than the AI systems currently being tested for driverless cars and in other Watson applications.

The huge advantage of an AI-FOMC would be both the capacity of the AI system to manage all historical records, both actions and results, plus ingest the very latest data and provide action continuously in fractions of a seconds instead of only eight times per year.

Google and others have developed, tested and accepted the fact that driverless cars will be in our foreseeable future. When all is said and done the AI system to replace the FOMC should be simpler than the AI systems now being tested for driverless cars.

The driverless, computer controlled cars have proven to be both safer and more efficient than human drivers. We can expect the same from an AI computer program designed to manage the nation's economy and money supply.

It should become an unnoticed background operation controlling our money supply, maintaining an active economy, providing full employment and a stable value of money and price stability. It can be done by bringing the full cadre of technologies together; communications, data accumulation, computer power, control system laws and economics and, most significant of all, AI technology.

The comparison with driverless cars is made, not because of a similarity of technical issues, but by the similarity of doubt in the general public.

A few years ago and in many conversations now, the notion of a driverless car would be met by laughs and derision. However, the concept has been proven in tests and the CEO of GM in a recent interview disclosed the strategy GM will employ in introducing computer driven cars in the future.

The computer driven cars have shown the power and versatility of AI equipped computer driven automatic controls. The process monitors the full environment and is much faster and precise than human operation of a vehicle.

Similar results can be expected from an AI equipped computer for the FOMC. The FOMC receives the regional bank reports and brings their individual experience and analytical talents to bear on considering actions to be taken based on the data in the reports. An AI computer program could access more data, more recent/real time data, access it faster and analyze it with greater precision than humans. It would operate continuously and not be limited in time response by the eight meetings per year observed by the Fed.

The parameters, specifications and characteristics of the AI system would and should be the subject of intense discussions. Replacing the FOMC and the money control system with a computer program will not be as simple as replacing a single car driver. The FOMC AI system would be replacing a system, not just a single individual performing a single function.

Additionally, the system that is being replaced has many pieces, each with its own features and characteristics. As noted in the previous chapter the system includes the reporting functions of the twelve regional Federal Reserve banks, the FOMC, commercial banks and the economy which borrows and repays loans. Government spending, taxing and borrowing is, at minimum, a transient part of the system even though its average effect on the money supply is zero.

The politics will be difficult as issues are identified and brought into focus. Do we really need a national debt? Do we need to rely on the "market" to determine the money supply? It has failed us many times. Should we then ditch the endogenous money supply notion? Should federal taxing and spending be an integral part of the system rather than just a transient player?

The top level design of an AI system to replace the FOMC should include a hard look at presently used tools and new tools that could be utilized by an AI system to control and manage the money supply and the economy. As noted previously, adjustments in the bank overnight interest rate and control of reserves by open market operations are weak tools and have failed in the recent 09 crash.

Government spending and taxing, obviously strong tools for money management, could be a part of the design. Borrowing or perhaps deposits in a national savings bank could also be a data point and a tool via interest rate adjustments, in the forward loop of the control system.

A new tool for automated money management is found in recently discussed economic ideas. The notion of a guaranteed job and income is socially and economically useful and offers a potentially strong tool for monetary management.

The payment system would obviously be automated with banking accounts being increased each month by the established stipend. The automated system could be a part of the negative feedback process in the AI driven control loop, the stipend being increased when economic activity slows and decreased when the economy heats up.

An assisting and fortuitous psychological result would be the "learning" by consumers that an increase in their monthly stipend means they should go shopping and a reduction means to hold off on consuming, making consumers an integral part of the control system loop.

Taxes should be an integral part of the money management system. They are not now as a rule although the congress has occasionally given "tax holidays" as an economic stimulus in slow economic times. Normal congressional reaction times are, however, totally incompatible with any meaningful control system.

In order to utilize taxing as a part of the control system, congress would need to establish ranges of taxes, not brackets, and allow the automated adjustment of taxes to become an integral part of the control system. The automated tax system could adjust taxes in response to economic conditions on weekly, perhaps daily bases, compared to the time scale associated with acts of congress.

A compatible tax code is discussed in Appendix G. It has been relegated to an appendix because it is very technical. A computer program has been created to illustrate how it would operate. The program is available to readers.

Government spending is and must remain the responsibility of congress and the constitution requires that all debts of the government must be paid. There is, however, some, perhaps significant in a control system sense, "wiggle room" in government spending to make it a tool for money management. The punctuality of payments could be an element in the control system.

Payments could be made faster in a slow economy and with more delay in a hot economy. A payment grace time of perhaps a week could provide strength to the spending tool in the control system.

In any control system speed is very important and its importance in monetary management is very obvious. In particular, it must be faster than the economy being controlled by way of the monetary aggregates. A system with the elements discussed above could easily maintain a sample rate of one per week and potentially one or two per day.

The beauty of a well designed AI control system is that it would work unnoticed in the background. Once the system "locks on" it will operate

on very small errors and disappear from the consci-
entiousness of users/benefactors of the system.
That would be the goal of the AI computer system
design.

Chapter 14

A Roadmap to Universal Healthcare

Healthcare costs in the USA in 2016 were 3.07 T$. With 126 million families in the nation, that is an average of $24,365.00 per family per year. The average family income was about $54,000.00 per year and 40% of families had incomes under $25,000.00 per year. It is obvious that, on average, American families cannot afford healthcare if they must pay for it with their income. Neither can they be expected to save an adequate amount to pay, on average, the cost of healthcare.

The federal government, through Medicare and Medicaid pay about 1.2 T$ per year of this cost and private insurance paid about 1.1 T$ and out of pocket expenditures were an estimated 0.3 T$.

The concept of a National Savings Bank was introduced in chapter ten. Enabling the establishment of a universal healthcare system is one of the potential benefits of establishing an NSB.   The

NSB, as described in chapter nine, would be the recipient of deposits equaling or exceeding the current national debt. Using these depository assets and conventional leveraging of times eight to twelve, the bank would be able to make loans equaling eight to twelve times the present national debt!

An NSB would provide numerous options for both establishing universal healthcare and simplifying the existing disjointed healthcare depository pools such as Medicare, Medicaid, VA healthcare and private funds established by corporations to finance healthcare for employees. All of these funds could be surrendered to a single pool in an NSB account and all healthcare costs could be paid out of the one pool.

The current apparatus for paying healthcare cost could remain in existence, including health insurance companies. Health insurance companies could sell policies with the cost of the policies being based on the operating cost of the company plus profits. This would establish real competition between insurance companies to minimize their operating cost for the administration of paying healthcare bills out of the single NSB pool.

Importantly, health insurance companies would not be incentivized to increase healthcare costs as they are now. Under the present system increasing healthcare costs results in higher sales, greater profits and larger executive salaries for healthcare insurance companies.

Shortfalls in funding of the pool could be covered by 100% seigniorage funding directly from the US Treasury. That is a simple statement but its implications are enormous.

-Appendix A-

TAXES FOR REVENUE ARE OBSOLETE

by: Beardsley Ruml
Chairman of the Federal Reserve Bank of New York.
[The following article was first published in the January, 1946 issue of a periodical named "American Affairs" and was copied from a posting in hiwaay.net.]

The superior position of public government over private business is nowhere more clearly evident than in government's power to tax business. Business gets its many rule-making powers from public government. Public government sets the limits to the exercise of these rule-making powers of business, and protects the freedom of business operations within this area of authority. Taxation is one of the limitations placed by government on the power of business to do what it pleases.

There is nothing reprehensible about this procedure. The business that is taxed is not a creature of flesh and blood, it is not a citizen. It has no voice in how it shall be governed --- nor should it. The issues in the taxation of business are not moral issues, but are questions of practical effect: What will get the best results? How should business be taxed so that business will make its greatest contribution to the common good?

It is sometimes instructive when faced with alternatives to ask the underlying question. If we are to understand the problems involved in the taxation of business, we must first ask: "Why does the government need to tax at all?" This seems to be a simple question, but, as is the case with simple questions, the obvious answer is likely to be a superficial one. The obvious answer is, of course, that taxes provide the revenue which the government needs in order to pay its bills.

It Happened

If we look at the financial history of recent years it is apparent that nations have been able to pay their bills even though their tax revenues fell short of expenses. These countries whose expenses were greater than their receipts from taxes paid their bills by borrowing the necessary money. The borrowing of money, therefore, is an alternative which governments use to supplement the revenues from taxation in order to obtain the necessary means for the payment of their bills.

A government which depends on loans and on the refunding of its loans to get the money it requires for its operations is necessarily dependent on the sources from which the money can be obtained. In the past, if a government persisted in borrowing heavily to cover its expenditures, interest rates would get higher and higher, and greater and greater inducements would have to be offered by the government to the lenders. These governments finally found that the only way they could maintain both their sovereign independence and their solvency was to tax heavily enough to meet a substantial part of their financial needs, and to be prepared ---if placed under undue pressure --- to tax to meet them all.

The necessity for a government to tax in order to maintain both its independence and its solvency is true for state and local governments, but it is not true for a national government. Two changes of the greatest consequence have occurred in the last twenty-five years which have substantially altered the position of the national state with respect to the financing of its current requirements.

The first of these changes is the gaining of vast new

experience in the management of central banks.

The second change is the elimination, for domestic purposes, of the convertibility of the currency into gold.

Free of the Money Market

Final freedom from the domestic money market exists for every sovereign national state where there exists an institution which functions in the manner of a modern central bank, and whose currency is not convertible into gold or into some other commodity.

The United States is a national state which has a central banking system, the Federal Reserve System, and whose currency, for domestic purposes, is not convertible into any commodity. It follows that our Federal Government has final freedom from the money market in meeting its financial requirements. Accordingly, the inevitable social and economic consequences of any and all taxes have now become the prime consideration in the imposition of taxes. In general, it may be said that since all taxes have consequences of a social and economic character, the government should look to these consequences in formulating its tax policy. All federal taxes must meet the test of public policy and practical effect. The public purpose which is served should never be obscured in a tax program under the mask of raising revenue.

What Taxes Are Really For

Federal taxes can be made to serve four principal purposes of a social and economic character. These purposes are:

1. As an instrument of fiscal policy to help stabilize the purchasing power of the dollar;

2. To express public policy in the distribution of wealth and of income, as in the case of the progressive income and estate taxes;

3. To express public policy in subsidizing or in penalizing various industries and economic groups;

4. To isolate and assess directly the costs of certain national benefits, such as highways and social security.

In the recent past, we have used our federal tax program consciously for each of these purposes. In serving these purposes, the tax program is a means to an end. The purposes themselves are matters of basic national policy which should be established, in the first instance, independently of any national tax program.

Among the policy questions with which we have to

deal are these:

Do we want a dollar with reasonably stable purchasing power over the years?

Do we want greater equality of wealth and of income than would result from economic forces working alone?

Do we want to subsidize certain industries and certain economic groups?

Do we want the beneficiaries of certain federal activities to be aware of what they cost?

These questions are not tax questions; they are questions as to the kind of country we want and the kind of life we want to lead. The tax program should be a means to an agreed end. The tax program should be devised as an instrument, and it should be judged by how well it serves its purpose.

By all odds, the most important single purpose to be served by the imposition of federal taxes is the maintenance of a dollar which has stable purchasing power over the years. Sometimes this purpose is stated as "the avoidance of inflation"; and without the use of federal taxation all other means of stabilization, such as monetary policy and price controls and subsidies, are unavailing. All other means, in any case, must be integrated with federal tax policy if we are to have tomorrow a dollar which has a value near to what it has today.

The war has taught the government, and the government have taught the people, that federal taxation has much to do with inflation and deflation, with the prices which have to be paid for the things that are bought and sold. If federal taxes are insufficient or of the wrong kind, the purchasing power in the hands of the public is likely to be greater than the output of goods and services with which this purchasing demand can be satisfied. If the demand becomes too great, the result will be a rise in prices, and there will be no proportionate increase in the quantity of things for sale. This will mean that the dollar is worth less than it was before --- that is inflation. On the other hand, if federal taxes are too heavy or are of the wrong kind, effective purchasing power in the hands of the public will be insufficient to take from the producers of goods and services all the things these producers would like to make. This will mean widespread unemployment.

The dollars the government spends become purchasing power in the hands of the people who have received them. The dollars the government takes by taxes cannot be spent by the people, and, therefore, these dollars can no longer be used to acquire the things which are available for sale. Taxation is, therefore, an instrument of the first importance in the administration of any fiscal and monetary policy.

To Distribute the Wealth

The second principal purpose of federal taxes is to attain more equality of wealth and of income than would result from economic forces working alone. The taxes which are effective for this purpose are the progressive individual income tax, the progressive estate tax, and the gift tax. What these taxes should be depends on public policy with respect to the distribution of wealth and of income. It is important, here, to note that the estate and gift taxes have little or no significance, as tax measures, for stabilizing the value of the dollar. Their purpose is the social purpose of preventing what otherwise would be high concentration of wealth and income at a few points, as a result of investment and reinvestment of income not expended in meeting day-to-day consumption requirements. These taxes should be defended and attacked it terms of their effects on the character of American life, not as revenue measures.

The third reason for federal taxes is to provide a subsidy for some industrial or economic interest. The most conspicuous example of these taxes is the tariffs on imports. Originally, taxes of this type were imposed to serve a double purpose since, a century and a half ago, the national government required revenues in order to pay its bills. Today, tariffs on imports are no longer needed for revenue. These taxes are nothing more than devices to provide subsidies to selected industries; their social purpose is to provide a price floor above which a domestic industry can compete with goods which can be produced abroad and sold in this country more cheaply except for the tariff protection. The subsidy is paid, not at the port of entry where the imported goods are taxed, but in the higher price level for all goods of the same type produced and sold at home.

The fourth purpose served by federal taxes is to assess, directly and visibly, the costs of certain benefits. Such taxation is highly desirable in order to limit the benefits to amounts which the people who benefit are willing to pay. The most conspicuous examples of such measures are the social security benefits, old-age and unemployment insurance. The social purposes of giving such benefits and of assessing specific taxes to meet the costs are obvious. Unfortunately and unnecessarily, in both cases, the programs have involved staggering deflationary consequences as a result of the excess of current receipts over current disbursements.

The Bad Tax

The federal tax on corporate profits is the tax which is most important in its effect on business operations. There are other taxes which are of great concern to special classes of business. There are many problems of state and local taxation of business which become extremely urgent, particularly when a corporation has no profits at all. However, we shall confine our discussion to the federal corporation income tax, since it is in this way that business is principally taxed. We shall also confine our considerations to the problems of ordinary peacetime taxation since, during wartime, many tax measures, such as the excess-profits tax, have a special justification.

Taxes on corporation profits have three principal consequences --- all of them bad. Briefly, the three bad effects of the corporation income tax are:

1. The money which is taken from the corporation in taxes must come in one of three ways. It must

come from the people, in the higher prices they pay for the things they buy; from the corporation's own employees in wages that are lower than they otherwise would be; or from the corporation's stockholders, in lower rate of return on their investment. No matter from which sources it comes, or in what proportion, this tax is harmful to production, to purchasing power, and to investment.

2. The tax on corporation profits is a distorting factor in managerial judgment, a factor which is prejudicial to clear engineering and economic analysis of what will be best for the production and distribution of things for use. And, the larger the tax, the greater the distortion.

3. The corporation income tax is the cause of double taxation. The individual taxpayer is taxed once when his profit is earned by the corporation, and once again when he receives the profit as a dividend. This double taxation makes it more difficult to get people to invest their savings in business than if the profits of business were only taxed once. Furthermore, stockholders with small incomes bear as heavy a burden under the corporation income tax as do stockholders with large incomes.

Analysis

Let us examine these three bad effects of the tax on corporation profits more closely. The first effect we observed was that the corporation income tax results in either higher prices, lower wages, reduced return on investment, or all three in combination. When the corporation income tax was first imposed it may have been believed by some that an impersonal levy could be placed on the profits of a soulless corporation, a levy which would be neither a sales tax, a tax on wages, or a double tax on the stockholder. Obviously, this is impossible in any real sense. A corporation is nothing but a method of doing business which is embodied in words inscribed on a piece of paper. The tax must be paid by one or more of the people who are parties at interest in the business, either as customer, as employee, or as stockholder.

It is impossible to know exactly who pays how much of the tax on corporation profits. The stockholder pays some of it, to the extent that the return on his investment is less than it would be if there were no tax. But, it is equally certain that the stockholder does not pay all of the tax on corporate income --- indeed, he may pay very little of it. After a period of time, the corporation income tax is figured as one of the costs of production and it gets passed on in higher prices charged for the company's goods and services, and in lower wages, including conditions of work which are inferior to what they otherwise might be.

The reasons why the corporation income tax is passed on, in some measure, must be clearly understood. In the operations of a company, the management of the business, directed by the profit motive, keeps its eyes on what is left over as profit for the stockholders. Since the corporation must pay its federal income taxes before it can pay dividends, the taxes are thought of --- the same as any other uncontrollable expense --- as an outlay to be covered by higher prices or lower costs, of which the principal cost is wages. Since all competition in the same line of business is thinking the same way, prices and costs will tend to stabilize at a point which will produce a profit, after taxes, sufficient to give the industry access to new capital at a reasonable price. When this finally happens, as it must if the industry is to hold its own, the federal income tax on corporations will have been largely absorbed in higher prices and in lower wages. The effect of the corporation income tax is, therefore, to raise prices blindly and to lower wages by an undeterminable amount. Both tendencies are in the wrong direction and are harmful to the public welfare.

Where Would the Money Go?

Suppose the corporation income tax were removed, where would the money go that is now paid in taxes? That depends. If the industry is highly competitive, as is the case with retailing, a large share would go in lower prices, and a smaller share would go in higher wages and in higher yield on savings invested in the industry. If labor in the industry is strongly organized, as in the railroad, steel, and automotive industries, the share going in higher wages would tend to increase. If the industry is neither competitive nor organized nor regulated --- of which industries there are very few --- a large share would go to the stockholders. In so far as the elimination of the present corporation income tax would result in lower prices, it would raise the standard of living for everyone.

The second bad effect of the corporation income tax is that it is a distorting factor in management judgment, entering into every decision, and causing actions to be taken which would not have been taken on business grounds alone. The tax consequences of every important commitment have to be appraised. Sometimes, some action which ought to be taken cannot be taken because the tax results make the transaction valueless, or worse. Sometimes, apparently senseless actions are fully warranted because of tax benefits. The results of this tax thinking is to destroy the integrity of business judgment, and to set up a business structure and tradition which does not hang together in terms of the compulsion of inner economic or engineering efficiency.

Premium on Debt

The most conspicuous illustration of the bad effect of tax consideration on business judgment is seen in the preferred position that debt financing has over equity financing. This preferred position is due to the fact that interest and rents, paid on capital used in business, are deductible as expense; whereas dividends paid are not. The result weighs the scales always in favor of debt financing, since no income tax is paid on the deductible costs of this form of capital. This tendency goes on, although it is universally agreed that business and the country generally would be in a stronger position if a much larger proportion of all investment were in common stocks and equities, and a smaller proportion in mortgages and bonds.

It must be conceded that, in many cases, a high

corporation income tax induces management to make expenditures which prudent judgment would avoid. This is particularly true if a long-term benefit may result, a benefit which cannot or need not be capitalized. The long-term expense is shared involuntarily by government with business, and, under these circumstances, a long chance is often well worth taking. Scientific research and institutional advertising are favorite vehicles for the use of these cheap dollars. Since these expenses reduce profits, they reduce taxes at the same time; and the cost to the business is only the margin of the expenditure that would have remained after the taxes had been paid --- the government pays the rest. Admitting that a certain amount of venturesome expenditure does result from this tax inducement, it is an unhealthy form of unregulated subsidy which, in the end, will soften the fibre of management and will result in excess timidity when the risk must be carried by the business alone.

The third unfortunate consequence of the corporation income tax is that the same earnings are taxed twice, once when they are earned and once when they are distributed. This double taxation causes the original profit margin to carry a tremendous burden of tax, making it difficult to justify equity investment in a new and growing business. It also works contrary to the principles of the progressive income tax, since the small stockholder, with a small income, pays the same rate of corporation tax on his share of the earnings as does the stockholder whose total income falls in the highest brackets. This defect of double taxation is serious, both as it affects equity in the total tax structure, and as a handicap to the investment of savings in business.

Shortly, an Evil

Any one of these three bad effects of the corporation income tax would be enough to put it severely on the defensive. The three effects, taken together, make an overwhelming case against this tax. The corporation income tax is an evil tax and it should be abolished.

The corporation income tax cannot be abolished until some method is found to keep the corporate form from being used as a refuge from the individual income tax and as a means of accumulating un-needed, un-invested surpluses. Some way must be devised whereby the corporation earnings, which inure to the individual stockholders, are adequately taxed as income of these individuals.

The weaknesses and dangers of the corporation income tax have been known for years, and an ill-fated attempt to abolish it was made in 1936 in a proposed undistributed profits tax. This tax, as it was imposed by Congress, had four weaknesses which soon drove it from the books. First, the income tax on corporations was not eliminated in the final legislation, but the undistributed profits tax was added on top of it. Second, it was never made absolutely clear, by regulation or by statute, just what form of distributed capitalization of withheld and reinvested earnings would be taxable to the stockholders and not to the corporation. Third, the Securities and Exchange Commission did not set forth special and simple regulations covering securities issued to capitalize withheld earnings. Fourth, the earnings of a corporation were frozen to a particular fiscal year, with none of the flexibility of the carry-forward, carry-back provisions of the present law.

Granted that the corporation income tax must go, it will not be easy to devise protective measures which will be entirely satisfactory. The difficulties are not merely difficulties of technique and of avoiding the pitfalls of a perfect solution impossible to administer, but are questions of principle that raise issues as to the proper locus of power over new capital investment.

Can the government afford to give up the corporation income tax? This really is not the question. The question is this: Is it a favorable way of assessing taxes on the people --- on the consumer, the workers and investors --- who after all are the only real taxpayers? It is clear from any point of view that the effects of the corporation income tax are bad effects. The public purposes to be served by taxation are not thereby well served. The tax is uncertain in its effect with respect to the stabilization of the dollar, and it is inequitable as part of a progressive levy on individual income. It tends to raise the prices of goods and services. It tends to keep wages lower than they otherwise might be. It reduces the yield on investment and obstructs the flow of savings into business enterprise.

-Appendix B-
The Colony of Virginia's Money Act, March 1760[17]

And whereas it is of the greatest importance to pre-serve the credit of the paper currency of this colo-ny, and nothing can contribute more to that end than a due care to satisfy the publick that the paper bills of credit, or treasury-notes, are properly sunk, according to the true intent and meaning of the several acts of assembly passed for emitting the same; and the establishing a regular method for this purpose may prevent difficulties and confusion in settling the publick accounts,... Be it therefore enacted, by the authority aforesaid, That Peyton Randolph, esquire, Robert Carter Nicholas, Benja-min Waller, Lewis Burwell and George Wythe, gen-tleman, or any three of them, be, and they are hereby appointed a committee, to examine at least twice in every year (and oftener, if thereto desired

---

[17] The history and an analysis of this colonial Virginia mon-etary system can be found here: http://as.vanderbilt.edu/econ/sempapers/grubb-paper.pdf

by the treasurer for the time being) all such bills of credit, or treasury-notes, redeemable on the first day of March, one thousand seven hundred and sixty five, as have been or shall be paid into the treasury, in discharge of the duties and taxes imposed by any former act of assembly; and upon receipt of the said bills or notes, the said committee shall give to the treasurer for the time being a certificate of the amount thereof, which shall avail the said treasurer in the settlements of his accounts as effectually, at all intents and purposes, as if he produced the said bills or notes themselves: And the said committee are hereby required and directed, so soon as they have given such certificate, to cause all such bills or notes to be burnt and destroyed.

-Appendix C-

Executive Order 6102
Requiring Gold Coin, Gold Bullion and Gold Certificates to Be Delivered to the Government
Issued by FDR, April 5, 1933

By virtue of the authority vested in me by Section 5 (b) of the Act of October 6, 1917, as amended by Section 2 of the Act of March 9, 1933, entitled "An Act to provide relief in the existing national emergency in banking, and for other purposes," in which amendatory Act Congress declared that a serious emergency exists, I, Franklin D. Roosevelt, President of the United States of America, do declare that said national emergency still continues to exist and pursuant to said section do hereby prohibit the hoarding of gold coin, gold bullion, and gold certificates within the continental United States by individuals, partnerships, associations and corporations and hereby prescribe the following regulations for carrying out the purposes of this order:

Section 1. For the purposes of this regulation, the term "hoarding" means the withdrawal and withholding of gold coin, gold bullion or gold certificates from the recognized and customary channels of trade. The term "person" means any individual, partnership, association or corporation.

Section 2. All persons are hereby required to deliver on or before May 1, 1933, to a Federal Reserve Bank or a branch or agency thereof or to any member bank of the Federal Reserve System all gold coin, gold bullion and gold certificates now owned by them or coming into their ownership on or before April 28, 1933, except the following:

(a) Such amount of gold as may be required for legitimate and customary use in industry, profession or art within a reasonable time, including gold prior to refining and stocks of gold in reasonable amounts for the usual trade requirements of owners mining and refining such gold.

(b) Gold coin and gold certificates in an amount not exceeding in the aggregate $100 belonging to any one person; and gold coins having a recognized special value to collectors of rare and unusual coins.

I Gold coin and bullion earmarked or held in trust for a recognized foreign Government or foreign central bank or the Bank for International Settlements.

(d) Gold coin and bullion licensed for other proper transactions (not involving hoarding) including gold coin and bullion imported for reexport or held pending action on applications for export licenses.

Section 3. Until otherwise ordered any person becoming the owner of any gold coin, gold bullion, or gold certificates after April 28, 1933, shall, within three days after receipt thereof, deliver the same in the manner prescribed in Section 2; unless such gold coin, gold bullion or gold certificates are held for any of the purposes specified in paragraphs (a), (b), or (c) of Section 2; or unless such gold coin or gold bullion is held for purposes specified in paragraph (d) of Section 2 and the person holding it is, with respect to such gold coin or bullion, a licensee or applicant for license pending action thereon.

Section 4. Upon receipt of gold coin, gold bullion or gold certificates delivered to it in accordance with Sections 2 or 3, the Federal Reserve Bank or member bank will pay therefor an equivalent amount of any other form of coin or currency coined or issued under the laws of the United States.

Section 5. Member banks shall deliver all gold coin, gold bullion and gold certificates owned or received by them (other than as exempted under the provisions of Section 2) to the Federal Reserve Banks of their respective districts and receive credit or payment therefor.

Section 6. The Secretary of the Treasury, out of the sum made available to the President by Section 501 of the Act of March 9, 1933, will in all proper cases pay the reasonable costs of transportation of gold coin, gold bullion or gold certificates delivered to a member bank or Federal Reserve Bank in accordance with Section 2, 3, or 5 hereof, including the cost of insurance, protection, and such other incidental costs as may be necessary, upon production of satisfactory evidence of such costs. Voucher forms for this purpose may be procured from Federal Reserve Banks.

Section 7. In cases where the delivery of gold coin, gold bullion or gold certificates by the owners thereof within the time set forth above will involve extraordinary hardship or difficulty, the Secretary of the Treasury may, in his discretion, extend the time within which such delivery must be made. Applications for such extensions must be made in writing under oath, addressed to the Secretary of the Treasury and filed with a Federal Reserve Bank. Each application must state the date to which the extension is desired, the amount and location of the gold coin, gold bullion and gold certificates in respect of which such application is made and the facts showing extension to be necessary to avoid extraordinary hardship or difficulty.

Section 8. The Secretary of the Treasury is hereby authorized and empowered to issue such further regulations as he may deem necessary to carry out the purposes of this order and to issue licenses thereunder, through such officers or agencies as he may designate, including licenses permitting the Federal Reserve Banks and member banks of the Federal Reserve System, in return for an equivalent amount of other coin, currency or credit, to deliver, earmark or hold in trust gold coin and bullion to or for persons showing the need for the same for any of the purposes specified in paragraphs (a), (c) and (d) of Section 2 of these regulations.

Section 9. Whoever willfully violates any provision of this Executive Order or of these regulations or of any rule, regulation or license issued there under may be fined not more than $10,000, or, if a natural person, may be imprisoned for not more than ten years, or both; and any officer, director, or agent of any corporation who knowingly participates in any such violation may be punished by a like fine, imprisonment, or both.

This order and these regulations may be modified or revoked at any time.

-Appendix D-
The Notion of Money

We use many things in our daily lives and, for the most part, we know what the things are AND we know how we can use them. And we don't confuse what we use them for with what they are. For example, a cell phone: We know it is made from metal, plastic and has electronics in it and that it uses radio waves from a tower someplace; that is what it is but we use it to talk to people (and sometimes computers these days) who are far away from us. It is the same with a car; it is made of metal, plastic, rubber and wires; it needs a battery and we have to pump in fuel but we use it to go from point "A" to point "B" if there is a passable road between the two points. What a thing is and what we use it for are two totally different things. But, unfortunately for us individually and perhaps our society as a whole, there is one thing we use on a daily bases with which we have troubles conceptualizing the difference between what it is and how we use it. Money. We are taught from the time we are toddlers what we can do with money. Ask anyone out of the blue "Do you know what money is?" and they will probably smile and say "Of course." But then press them with "Well, what is money?" and they might frown, think a little and then respond, "Well, you can buy stuff and pay bills with money." Right. That is how you use it. Now, what is this money, totally divorced from how you can use it? That's a much harder question[18].

Many noteworthy people have commented on this basic ignorance about what money really is. Henry Ford made a famous comment concerning money. He said: "It is well enough that people of the nation do not understand our banking and money system, for if they did, I believe there would be a revolution before tomorrow morning."[19] My intention is not to instigate a revolution but I do want to do my part to inform. I agree with the observation of another wise but controversial person, Ezra Pound, who opined that the social conse-

---

[18] The notion that money is paper with green ink is not worth pursuing nor, pieces of metal nor marks on computer disks...

[19] This and many other quotes on banking and money can be found at this URL: http://www.themoneymasters.com/the-money-masters/famous-quotations-on-banking/

quences of the world population fully understanding money would compare with the experienced consequences of the world population generally becoming literate, which were, as we know, truly enormous.

The literature is replete with good articles and books on money, what it is and what is wrong with our current monetary system. These books, articles and observations stretch back from the present day to near pre-history. Even Jesus is quoted as giving an insightful observation when he advised someone to "give unto Caesar what is Caesar's and unto God what is God's"[20], noting that money is really the property of the state; that we are only using it. I cannot claim originality for much of the material given here; I am only offering my point of view and the results of my thinking and analysis, hoping to help bring about that time when we all have a better understanding of money and can use that understanding for the betterment of our world community rather than having it used as a tool for the creation of individual and group power.

We can start our quest to understand money

---

[20] Mark 12:17

by considering why there is such a thing as money. Why was it needed? How did it come into being? A real hermit would not need money. Living alone and out of contact with other people he would never need nor have an opportunity to use money. Likewise, a very individualistic and conservative person who can build his own shelter, provide for his own food and make his own clothes would not have a real need for money. He would only need money if he wanted things or services provided by others.

From these observations we can see that money is coupled with living with other people, living in a community and depending on others to provide some parts of our needs while we, in turn, supply some of the needs of others. Money, then, is the enabler of a collective society where people depend on each other to supply their needs and diverse desires. It is important to note the collective society enabled by money is not necessarily akin to the one described by Biddle[21] who is more interest-

---

[21] "Individualism vs. Collectivism: Our Future, Our Choice" by Craig Biddle, http://www.craigbiddle.com/articles.htm

ed in current liberal vs. conservative notions. Here, in my references, a "collective society" is merely one where people depend on the labor of others to satisfy their needs and desires. Both societies described by Biddle meet this definition. In fact from all that we know about man and his evolution through pre-history, we have always been a collective society. Even cave man had his artists who ate, lived and thrived while someone in his collective group provided him food and shelter. Hence, it is fair to say, we as humans cannot conceive of a society that is not a collective society, where people depend on the labors of others to provide some of their needs and desires while, in turn, they also provide to others using their own capabilities.

One change through history has been the evolution of the size of the collective group. Grouping probably started with family groups then grew to tribes and evolved under strong leaders to groups of tribes finally becoming states and nations as we have today. The fuel for this ever expanding size of groups has been transportation and communication. And it is not an overstatement to suggest we have reached very near the pinnacle in both areas with fast, world spanning transport and earth spanning communications. Both transportation and communications will, without doubt, improve with technical advances and development over the coming years but we now have the basis for a worldwide, collective society. Our current struggles with international trade and the interplay of monetary systems attest to the efforts to make the worldwide collective society work. But the people involved in this daunting work to enable international trade and solve monetary conflicts would not define their goal as creating a global collective society. They might even be peeved to be accused of such an activity but that, very definitely, is what they are doing. Sometimes you need to look down and back in order to see forward and up.

Another change/evolution has been the increased diversity of things we depend on others to supply to us and for which we use money to secure. A century and a half ago the important things requiring money were very limited compared to the highly diverse things and services now available in the market place. This increased diversity of commodities and services acquired with money obscures the basic function and original need for money. We can fail to see money as a tool to enable us to live with others and depend on them for our needs and, in turn, their dependence on our own productive work to supply something of value to others in our lives.

If we accept the notion that money is the enabler of a collective society where people depend on each other for their livelihood requirements then we do make money a commodity with ethereal qualities. How many movements, rally's, speeches, inspirational courses and organizations have the objective to achieve a society where people depend on each other and care for each other? Could we say every religion we understand and perhaps those we do not fully comprehend have as a goal "the brotherhood of man" and respect and service for others? Could it be that this stuff we call money is the key to attaining these lofty goals proclaimed by noble persons throughout history? An admonition about money well known to us is given in **First Timothy 6:10, "For the love of money is the root of all kinds of evil." And it can be but it does not have to be.**

The academic study of money is relegated to a portion of the subject of economics and economics describes itself as an "inexact" science. This assertion may be the only completely acceptable statement to ever be made by an economist. The field of economics is often overfilled with attempts to justify existing practices in business and in banking and is all too willing to bypass logic in order to make these justifications in their "inexact" way. One such justification is about the creation of money. Economists state and all too many people believe that banks "create" money. However simple logic, a Gedanken experiment, disproves this assertion. In our monetary system, banks do not create money. Making entries into a journal do not make money. The existence of the FDIC is a testament to the fact banks do not create money. The law making it a federal crime to advocate making runs on banks is another statement that banks do not create money. Bottom line, banks use money but they do not create money in our system.

The question "What is money?" becomes much easier to answer when we apply logic to the issue and discount the fables such as the creation of money by banks. If we discount the other head scratching assertions that "credit" and "debt" are money then we can understand what money in our system really is. It is a commodity, a very inexpensive commodity, produced by the Bureau of Engraving and Printing (BEP) in the US Treasure Department of our government and the coins produced by the US Mints. It is inexpensive because the BEP produces a $100.00 bill for just 9.7 cents.[22] Coins are more expensive to produce and lower denomination bills have a higher cost to value ratio. The 100s were less expensive to produce until a more sophisticated process was applied in recent years to foil counterfeiters. A new $100 is promised in the later months of 2013 and it will probably be more sophisticated and costly to produce.

Money is then a bartering commodity with a widely accepted value. It simplifies the bartering process with the buyer having a commodity of accepted value to exchange for the sellers commodity or service at the price offered by the seller. Money simplifiers the bartering process by requiring only the buyer to evaluate the value of the offered item rather than both parties having to evaluate the value of the item offered by the other.

---

[22] The distinction between these two forms of money, so called "bills" and coins or specie, is important and very interesting too but would be a tangential diversion from our central question concerning money.

Many will disagree with the assertion that banks do not create money. But simple logic easily shows they do not. Go through the process of getting a $1000.00 loan at a bank where you have an account. The bank official does the two entries, one in your account showing you have an additional $1000.00. Write a check to yourself and go cash it at a teller. The teller will hand you $1000.00. Then ask the question, "Did this cash just appear when I got the loan or was it here before?"

The answer is obvious, the cash was there before the loan was made in the tellers drawer or stored away as vault cash. The loan process did not create the money. The loan process only gave you access to cash the bank was already holding. And the bank does not have the money really to loan to you. They will probably have 80.00 in reserve to "back up" the 1000.00 they loaned you, assuming a nominal 8% reserve requirement. So what is the bank doing using this fractional reserve process? They are engaging in this most ancient fraud developed by banks ages ago and still being used to this day. Why is it fraud? Look at the definition[23] of fraud. That is precisely what banks do in the loan process. Those who claim banks create money by the fractional reserve loan process are being shrills for banks, trying to legitimize an obviously fraudulent process. Banks don't create money, they draw interest on money they do not have.

The above is a micro view of money as it is used by banks. Turning now to a macro view we encounter the most important obligation of managers of a monetary system; to provide the proper amount of money into an economic entity. The proper amount is usually defined in terms of its effect on the economy, not by a precise amount. The proper amount will provide a low unemployment rate which has been defined as "full employment" and will sustain an economy with stable prices; that is, neither inflation nor deflation is occurring. You

---

[23] fraud /frôd/ Noun
Wrongful or criminal deception intended to result in financial or personal gain.
A person or thing intended to deceive others, typically by unjustifiably claiming or being credited with accomplishments or qualities.

may want to pause and read that again. It is fact. The independent monetary authorities have the power of employment/unemployment and inflation/deflation by controlling the money supply.

Now, let's look at some money supply data. The curve shown below tells us a lot. A mathematician's eye will see an exponential curve. He would like to see an expanded scale plot for the 1913 to 1939 data to understand that period better. We can also see the very obvious bump up in 1940 at the onset of WWII. Those of us old enough to remember know what happened as the going to war economy boomed and everyone was working to support the war effort. People said the war caused the economy to pick up[24] but the real reason was a buildup of money spurring the economy.

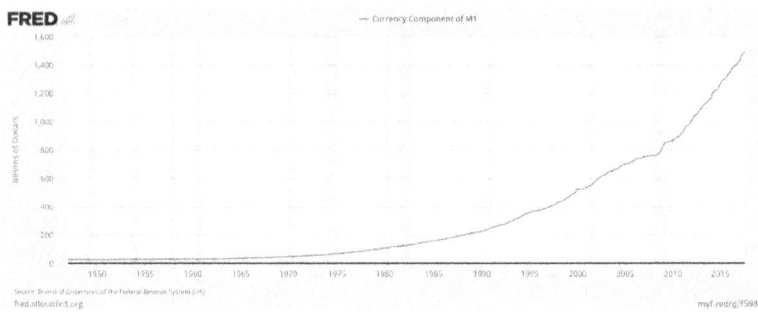

Figure 1 Historical Data: Money In Circulation

---

[24]See:http://www.shmoop.com/wwii-home-front/economy.html

There is a very prominent peak near 2000 that is well explained in the literature[25] by the boom and bust of the "dot com" bubble. Another feature in the curve is the short flat segment near 2008 near 800 billion followed by a very sharp rise in 2009. Before discussing that subject we need to look at some features of our monetary system.

We have had many monetary systems in our country. One of the oldest and the longest enduring one was the use of bales of tobacco for money. Tobacco was an important export product and had an acknowledged value. Tobacco was used as money for over 140 years during the colonial period and it proved Gresham's[26] law again. Plantation owners sold or smoked and chewed their best tobacco and used the least valuable as money. The Articles of Confederation (1781) did not contain any specific

---

[25]See:
http://inflationdata.com/Inflation/Inflation/Money_Supply_and_Inflation.asp

[26] Gresham's Law states that money with the least intrinsic or perceived value will circulate.
http://en.wikipedia.org/wiki/Gresham's_law

definition of a monetary system for the new nation but did give Congress the power to define coins[27] by alloy and value. It has been rumored that the nature of the nation's monetary system was a hotly debated issue during the creation of the Constitution that replaced the Articles of Confederation ten years later in 1791. Again, the rumors are the delegates creating the Constitution agreed to disagree on a specific monetary system and again left the burden on the shoulders of the Congress, giving them again the power to coin money[28] and set the value thereof.

Congress acted quickly, chartering the First US Bank in 1791 for a period of 20 years. Alexandria Hamilton, who was Secretary of the Treasure for President Washington, was the primary backer of the new bank, using the Bank of England as a model. Prominent persons, Thomas Jefferson and James

---

[27] "The United States in Congress assembled shall also have the sole and exclusive right and power of regulating the alloy and value of coin struck by their own authority, or by that of the respective States --..."

[28] Article I, Section 8: " The Congress shall have Power To...... coin Money, regulate the Value thereof, and of foreign Coin, and fix the Standard of Weights and Measures;..."

Madison, were opposed but Washington finally signed the "bank law".

The charter was not renewed in 1811 and over a period of 6 years there was no US central bank. The second US Bank was chartered in 1817 again hotly debated between industrial interests who favored the bank and agrarian representatives who opposed it. It was also charted for 20 years and again, in the famous "bank war" of Andrew Jackson, the charter of the second bank was not renewed. From that date in 1836 the US would not have a central bank again for 77 years when the Federal Reserve System was born in Dec of 1913. Over the 100 years of the Fed's life time many very significant things have happened resulting in great impacts on the central bank system. Some of these changes have been very visible and have been vigorously debated while others have been overlooked and just became "a part of the system." One very positive change the Fed brought to the nation's monetary system was to establish a uniform currency. In the preceding national banking era each bank designed their own notes, leading to confusions and difficulties described succinctly in an article[29] by the Philadelphia Fed:

> "Allowing each state bank to issue its own banknotes created its own set of problems. For one thing, such a profusion of currency — with different sizes and different designs — could be confusing. For another thing — and perhaps more important — banknotes exchanged at a discount, meaning that they did not necessarily trade at face value. For example, in 1842, a $1 note from a Tennessee bank exchanged for 80 cents in Philadelphia; likewise, a $1 note from an Illinois bank exchanged for just 50 cents. The amount of the discount sometimes depended on the distance between the issuing bank and the paying bank and sometimes on perceptions of how sound the issuing bank was. In fact, discounts..."

The Federal Reserve Act, which was an agreement between bankers and congressional representatives, included provisions for the government to print notes for all banks, to be distributed by the Fed, thereby establishing a uniform national currency.

This responsibility resulted in the formation of the Bureau of Engraving and Printing (BEP) as a part of the Treasury Department. Establishing uniformity of bank notes was probably the first posi-

---

[29] The complete article can be read here:
http://philadelphiafed.org/publications/economic-education/state-and-national-banking-eras.pdf

tive result of the formation of the Fed. These notes were just paper, showing how much "real money" a bank owed to the bearer of the note. They remained "just paper" for about 20 years, until FDR in 1933 removed the gold backing of the notes. Gold backing is still a vigorously debated subject today but little debate has occurred on the subject of the BEP now selling real money to the Fed for the cost of printing.

The issue is seigniorage, the difference between the cost of producing money and the face value thereof. It is a very simple concept but, in order to explain away the government printing and selling money at cost to banks, a sophisticated "fairy tale"[30] has been developed about the rebates the Fed gives to the US Treasure based on interest they collect on their holdings of the national debt. The "cover story" for seigniorage of Federal Reserve notes has been contrived. To fully understand the nature of real seigniorage we need to look at the options available for a national monetary system which are discussed and described below.

The US currently has two separate and dis-

---

[30] See for example: http://en.wikipedia.org/wiki/Seigniorage

tinct monetary systems in operation, coins and paper notes, and they work together in a seamless fashion. Coins are minted by US mints and placed in the governments account at face value regardless of the cost of minting the coins. The seigniorage for pennies and nickels is negative; it costs more to mint them than their face value. The other coins have positive seigniorage; a quarter costs just 11 cents to mint and dollar coins are minted for just 18 cents.

Paper notes, on the other hand, are printed by the US Treasure's Bureau of Engraving and Printing (BEP) and then sold to the Federal Reserve for the cost of printing. A $100 bill costs just 9.7 cents to print and it is printed with great sophistication to foil counterfeiters. It is informative to follow a $100 bill through a potential lifetime. The bill is printed by the BEP, sold to the Fed for 9.7 cents and then potentially used by a bank to buy a government bond. Assume it is a 10 year, 6% per year bond. The government then must tax citizens $6 per year for 10 years to pay interest on the $100 and then tax for the full $100 to repay the loan. In the cycle citizens are taxed $160.00 so the government could borrow and repay $100 that the government originally sold to the banks for 9.7 cents. Alternatively, the government could have printed the bill and spent it to pay a government expense, paying a $100 debt for a cost of 9.7 cents to citizens. That is 1,650 times less if the government had taken the full seigniorage instead of passing it on, thereby increasing the wealth of banks.

There are no political discussions of the question of the government printing and spending money into the economy to pay its bills versus borrowing money, paying interest and collecting taxes to pay its bills. The subject is anathema in our politics. It is anathema because it is such a threat to the power and wealth of the banks and financial sector generally as the numbers above show. Politicians are afraid to discuss the subject, afraid because of the power of banks to retaliate for any suggestion that a sovereign government should issue money into its economy rather than allowing privately owned, for profit banks the unique privilege of issuing the national currency into circulation. But it is a discussion that is needed and needed now for many reasons.

A discussion of the nations monetary system would be classed as "boring" and "confusing" to many. One reason for that is that no one alive today remembers any monetary system other than the 100 year old Fed. The Fed is accepted by many as the only way for a monetary system to work. Another stumbling block is the disconnect between the value of money to us as individuals versus the cost to produce the money. While slipping a crisp $100 bill into our wallet it is hard to grasp the fact, and the significance of the fact, that the $100 bill cost the government only 9.7 cents to make. But it is a fact and it is a very significant fact.

The BEP, a very efficient and highly developed operation, produces about 1.5B$ per day with a majority of the production being 1$ bills. They claim about 90% of the production is used to replace worn/torn/unusable bills culled out by the daily activities of the Fed. This means the Fed is shredding and burning over 1B$ in cash each day. What does all of this mean? First, it obviously means that money is a very inexpensive commodity and that the US Treasury's BEP is very good at making it. The second point is less obvious; that the inexpensive nature of money is very good news for the government, for our economy and for our way of life. The discussion needed about the monetary system is to first explore and understand these advantages of inexpensive money, second, to explore why our present monetary system, the Fed, blocks us from enjoying these benefits and third, to understand the structure of a monetary system that will enable us to fully enjoy the personal and community benefits of inexpensive fiat currency.

Many readers at this point will be saying "Wait a minute, the government can't just print money and spend it because that will make the money worthless." And that observation is true and it is true for any monetary system, not just a government run monetary system. It points up the single most important feature of any monetary system; how the total supply of money is controlled to provide an adequate supply to sustain employment and the economy but not too much to create inflation and debasement of the currency.

Supplying too little money to an economy is an oppression of the citizens, robbing them of the ability to help each other by the free exchange of money for goods and services. Putting too much money into the economy leads to the frustration of increasing prices plus the debasement of savings. Unfortunately, both of these conditions can benefit certain groups in a community. A well designed monetary system must guard against being used to inflict either of these conditions on an economy for the benefit of a select few.

There are historical examples of both too much and too little money in an economy. An example of too much money in circulation is Nazi Germany in the '30s. The hyperinflation was created to enable Germany to pay reparations demanded by the allies following Germany's defeat in WWI. It worked. Germany paid off the reparations but at the expense of the frustration and pain of the German people suffering through the hyperinflation. And the world learned. Following WWII the Marshall Plan was devised to assist the defeated nations in rebuilding their economies and rejoining the community of nations rather than imposition of reparations.

We in the USA have experienced the "too-little-money" in circulation syndrome. It happened during the great depression of the '30s and it has happened again in the 2008 downturn. The visible indicators of the situation are copious signs of property for sale, real estate, homes, cars and many other items. People are forced to sell their property to obtain cash money and they are forced to sell at ever lower prices. There is a whispered name for this situation among those benefited by it. It is a "liquidation phase" where people are forced to sell property because of the sacristy of money imposed by the monetary system.

Both property and labor are liquidated when too little money is in the economy. Workers must liquidate their labor by working for ever lower wages. The groups who benefit from this situation are obvious. Those with saved money can purchase property at lower prices and employers can hire workers at lower wages. A well designed monetary system must be designed and policed to prevent it from being used to create either of these conditions; hyperinflation and debasement of the money supply or from the oppression of the population by an inadequate supply of money.

The tools available to a monetary system to control the money supply are an important consideration. A comparison can be made between our current monetary system, the privately owned central bank model we call the Federal Reserve and a government controlled monetary system. The Fed is charged by law with maintaining the money supply to avoid inflation and enable full employment. The primary tool it has to accomplish this task is buying and selling of government debt making a government debt necessary for operation of the central bank. Buying government debt puts money into bank reserves enabling banks to make more loans there by increasing the supply of money. The procedure can be reversed to reduce the money supply. It is a back door method depending on bond sellers to make deposits in American banks and depending on banks to make more loans when their reserves are increased. It is also a slow acting method, requiring many months to be felt in the economy.

The need for a national debt to support open market operations (as the process of buying and selling of government debt by the Fed is called) is very real as was shown during the late 1990s. The budget surpluses and projected debt reductions in the later part of the 90s under President Clinton frightened the monetary community with the prospect of a mortal blow to the Fed by having the national debt totally retired. The problem was "fixed" under the following Bush administration by the Bush tax cuts and expenditures on the war on terror.

Maintaining a stable money supply to serve the nation and the economy is a responsibility of the central bank. The oft stated target by the Fed for a "stable" supply is a growth rate of 3% per year.

Over the 100 year life of the Fed that would be a 19x increase in the money supply. The actual increase has been much larger. According to the Cleveland Fed (wp1304.pdf), currency in circulation in 1914 was 1.85B$ and in 2013 the number is 1.6T$, a real increase of 864 times or an average rate of 7% per year.

A quietly held secret of the Fed is that a steady, inflationary, compound interest-like growth in the money supply is a necessary result of the central bank monetary system model. Historical data confirms it as fact as noted above. The money supply versus years plot shown above can be modeled accurately by compounded interest at a nominal rate of 7% per year.

The reason for this is not difficult to understand. When banks loan a quantity of money into the economy for a period of time, say one year, then they must loan the same amount plus interest on the previous amount in order to maintain the money supply. If they don't loan this ever increasing amount the money supply shrinks, unemployment mounts and foreclosures on loans must occur because of the simple fact that not enough money is available in the economy to repay previous loans at interest.

This guaranteed inflationary character of the central bank model is often justified by the assertion that a government operated monetary system, where money is issued into the economy by government spending, is inflationary. The fact is the exact opposite. In a government operated monetary system, where money is issued by spending, it does not have to be returned as with loans and importantly, with no interest attached to them. This enables establishment of a non-inflationary, stable money supply.

Evidence of this fact can be seen in Figure 1, above. There is the ramp up of the money supply in the early '40s to accommodate the expenses of WWII followed by a very stable period reaching into the '60s. During this period the government introduced US Notes into the economy by direct spending to pay for the costs of the war. The issuing of US

Notes stopped Jan 21, 1971.

It is noteworthy that the US economy was booming in the war years and the years after. It was not a coincidence that these economic boom years occurred during a period of government spending of US Notes and a period when 100s of thousands of young men and women were given free college educations under the "GI Bill".

The Reconstruction Finance Corporation (RFC) was also in operation during this period. It was a government organized bank, the largest bank in the world at the time, putting the USA on a war footing after the attack on Pearl Harbor. The RFC, reviewed in detail in Appendix I [31], was an off budget credit agency that obtained funding directly from the US Treasury. Originally chartered under Hoover in 1933, it was used extensively during the FDR years and especially during WWII to develop the productive capacity in the nation to prevail in that great war.

A government operated monetary system, in addition to being free of the mandatory inflation of

---

[31] By James Butkiewicz, University of Delaware with editing for brevity

a central bank system, also has better and faster tools to manage and control the money supply. The money supply can be increased directly by spending or reduction in taxes compared to the indirect methods of the central bank; buying of government debt and adjustments to bank to bank interest rates.

The government can reduce and slow the growth of the money supply by reduced spending, increased taxes and by borrowing money, all very direct methods. Both the directness and the speed of the money supply control tools available to the government recommends them for the task of management of the money supply rather than a private group such as the Federal Reserve with only slow, indirect tools.

Our present situation in the US is a great case in point. Consider the construction industry, its un-employment status and the countries well known, crumbling infrastructure of roads, bridges and buildings. A recent figure for unemployment in the construction industry was 8.5% in a work force of 5.8 million or about 500,000 people. Think about what those 500,000 workers could accomplish over a period of two years repairing our crumbling roads and bridges. It would be enormous. And how much would it cost tax payers? We have to remember that if those construction workers get busy then many others get busy too supplying materials to those workers and responding to their increased demand for goods they can afford now that they have a job. It would be an economic boom. Now, the cost. Let's make a guess, maybe high, maybe low but say $200,000 per year for two years for 500,000 workers. That's a total of 200B$ into an economy that currently has 1,200B$ in circulation. That is a big increase in the money supply, about 17% but what effect would it have? Let's assume it is issued by the US Treasury under the Legal Tender Act of 1862 as "lawful money", the term applied to currency issued directly by the US Treasury, also referred to as "US Notes".

These US Notes would not cause inflation because they cannot, under law, be used as reserves by banks and multiplied by a factor of 8 to 12 times by fractional reserve loans. The US Notes are also called an "inelastic" currency for this reason. And getting back to how much it would cost tax payers, we can use the current printing cost of a $100 Federal Reserve note as a guide. A $100 bill costs less than 10 cents to print, a 1000:1 ratio called **seigniorage**. So the actual cost to tax payers would be, more or less, a paltry, insignificant 200M$.

With about 200M$ we put a million unemployed Americans to work, giving them a new lease on life. We get a bustling economy, we get a renewed infrastructure, repaired bridges, roads and buildings which will be a very real increase in the wealth of the nation provided by the labor of a half million now unemployed citizens. And a last, very real benefit: that 200B$ spent into the economy is a unique currency. It accrues no interest and does not have to be "paid back" as fed notes do, providing a continuing, stable money supply that can be used by citizens to enjoy the labor of others in exchange for their own chosen labor. So, why isn't it done? Would anyone be hurt? It looks like the citizens of the country and the nation at large would all win. Yes, but some would be hurt and suffer a very significant hurt. That 200B$ of lawful money placed into the economy and staying in the economy will "rob" banks of a nominal 14B$ per year(assuming a nominal 7% loan interest), **every year** as long as the US Notes remain in the economy because banks will not be required to loan the funds at interest that are already in the economy.

This is obviously why, very quietly, the issuance of US Notes was curtailed as of Jan 21, 1971. The trajectory of our economy from that date may, at least in part, be due to that curtailment of the issuance of US Notes. Of great importance here is that the purpose of this discussion is not to punish banks or "get back" at them or to take away their historical privileges. The reasons are pragmatic and are based on the competitive position of the country in the world, the health of the economy and the welfare and standard of living of the citizens of the country.

-Appendix E-
An Analysis of Bank Policy Options

Two options for bank lending policy will be examined. The first is for the bank to loan the same amount each year and the second will be a policy to make loans in a way that maintains a fixed amount of money in the active economy. In each case it is assumed no other sources of new money for the economy are used. Specifically, no government sovereign spending nor central bank open market operations are used to alter the quantity of money in the economy. The analysis will, thereby, show the actions needed by the central bank and/or the federal government to maintain stability in the economy.

The analysis recognizes that the bank has operational expenses which result in a part of earned interest being paid back into the economy. It is assumed that the balance of earned interest will result in an increase in the wealth of the bank over time.

If the bank does not save a portion of its earnings into reserves then it will not grow because greater reserves mean greater amounts can be loaned. Factual history shows that successful banks do grow and increase their reserves over time. Defining the following variables:

$R_0(y)$ = Bank reserves, 12/31/y

M_e = Money[32] in economy, 12/31/y

L = Constant loan amount on 1/1/y

M_0 = Initial money in economy

y = year

$i_t = i_r + i_e$: Total interest is interest placed in reserves plus interest portion returned to economy for bank operating expenses.

Assume the loan, L, is made on Jan 1st of each year and repaid on Dec 31st of the same year, then at the end of year y:

$M_e(y) = M_0 - L*i_r*y$ and,

$R_0(y) = R_0 + L*i_r*y$

$M_e(y)$ will be zero when: $y = M_0/(L*i_r)$ Recognizing the ratio L/M_0 is the ratio of loan amount to total money in the economy, we can write:

---

[32] This is the amount of free or sovereign money in the economy, coins, US Notes, Silver Certificates, etc, i.e. money not owed to nor created by banks.

$$y_x = L_f/i_r$$

where L_f is the ratio of total money in the economy to the amount of the annual loan made by the bank. Then y_x is the year at which all money has been removed from the economy into bank reserves.

Since 1934 bank assets have risen exponentially at 7.4% per year, Figure A-1. Assuming bank loans are equal to free money in the economy then the catastrophe of zero money in the economy would occur in approximately 13.4 years. It is clear that a bank policy of making fixed loans per unit time is unsustainable without sovereign spending by the federal government into the economy and/or monetization of the national debt by the central bank in order to replenish money in the economy.

Banks have another option; to make loans in such a way that the amount of money in the economy remains constant. Banks can accomplish this goal by always loaning back an amount equal to the previous loan plus the amount added to reserves from the previous loan.

The same notations used above can be used for this option except now the loan amount, L, will be a function of time, L(y).

The loan amount sequence is as follows:

YEAR	Loan Amount
1	L
2	$L*(1+i_r)$
3	$L*(1+i_r)*(1+i_r)$
4	$L*(1+i_r)*(1+i_r)*(1+i_r)$

The expression for L as a function of time is obvious:

$$L(y) = L*(1 + ir)^{y-1}$$

an exponential as shown in Figure A-2.

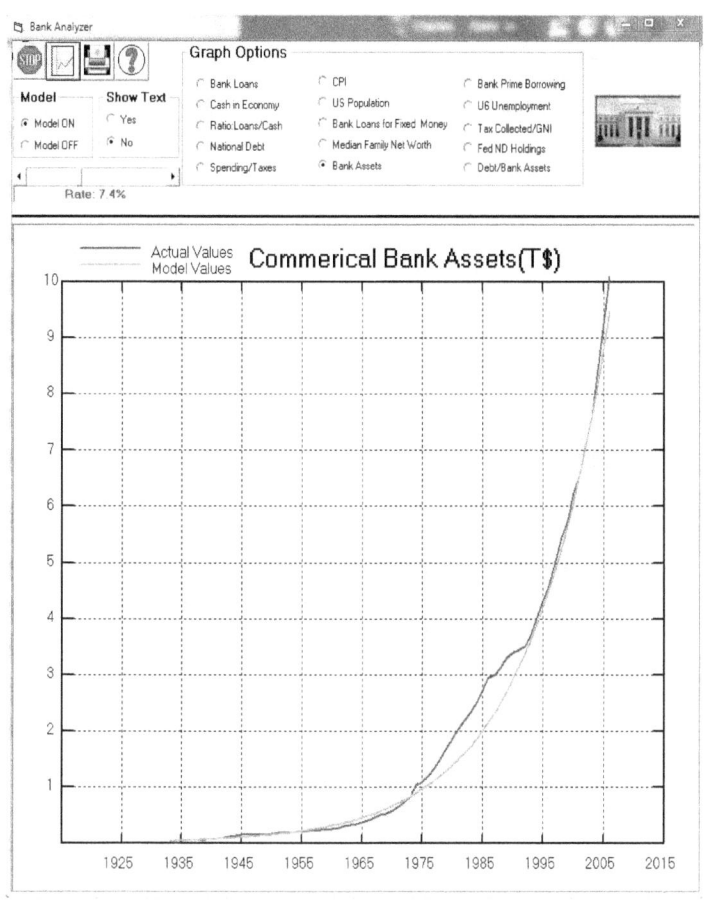

Figure A-1: Bank Assets

The crisis point will be reached when:

$$MO = L*(1 + i_r)^{Y_x-1}$$

Solving for y_x,

$$y_x = [\log(MO/L) / \log(1 + i_r)] + 1$$

Using $i_r = 0.074$ as before,

$$y_x = 32.3*\log(MO/L) + 1$$

The following table shows values of y_x for various ratios of MO/L.

MO/L	y_x (years)
100	65.6
10	33.3
5	23.6
2	10.7
1.5	6.8

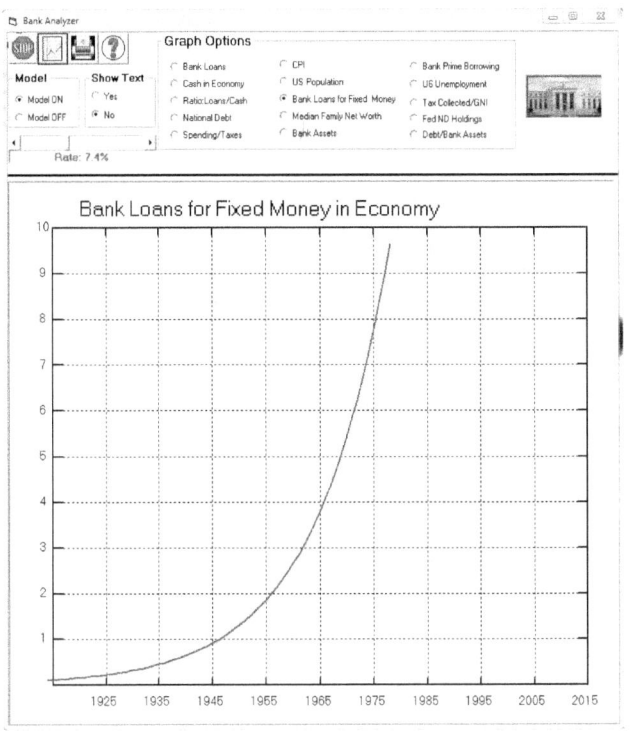

Figure A-2: Bank Loans for Fixed Money Supply

In the previous option the crises was from reduction of money in the economy. In this case the size of the loans will increase until the amount required to pay back the loans is greater than the total money in the economy. When this occurs there will be widespread defaults on loans as were experienced in the recent crash in '08.

-Appendix F-

The Federal Reserve's "Dual Mandate":
The Evolution of an Idea

By Aaron Steelman

Since 1977, the Federal Reserve has operated under a mandate from Congress to "promote effectively the goals of maximum employment, stable prices, and moderate long term interest rates"—what is now commonly referred to as the Fed's "dual mandate." The idea that the Fed should pursue multiple goals can be traced back to at least the 1940s, however, with shifting emphasis on which objective should be paramount. That such a mandate may, at times, create tensions for monetary policy has long been recognized as well.

At the conclusion of World War II, with millions of American soldiers returning home, a large share of the workforce concerned about finding jobs as the economy transitioned from the production of wartime goods, and the specter of the Great Depression fresh in the minds of nearly all, Congress passed the Employment Act of 1946. At the heart of the Act was its "Declaration of Policy":

The Congress hereby declares that it is the continuing policy and responsibility of the federal government to use all practicable means consistent with its needs and obligations and other essential considerations of national policy with the assistance and cooperation of industry, agriculture, labor, and State and local governments, to coordinate and utilize all its plans, functions, and resources for the purpose of creating and maintaining, in a manner calculated to foster and promote free competitive enterprise and the general welfare, conditions under which there will be afforded useful employment, for those able, willing, and seeking work, and to promote maximum employment, production, and purchasing power.[1]

The Act was the product of numerous revisions to what was originally introduced as the "Full Employment Bill of 1945." It had declared:

All Americans able to work and seeking work have the right to useful, remunerative, regular, and full-time employment, and it is the policy of the United States to assure the existence at all times of sufficient employment opportunities to enable all Ameri-

cans who have finished their schooling and who do not have full-time housekeeping responsibilities to freely exercise this right.[2]

Conspicuous in the final bill is the removal of the claim that citizens have a "right" to a job; so, too, is the acknowledgment of the importance of maintaining purchasing power—that is, the need to keep inflation in check. Political scientist Stephen Kemp Bailey attributed such changes, in large measure, to opposition among certain members of the House of Representatives who viewed the original bill as too radical and wished to produce a substitute that would "exclude the last remnants of … dangerous federal commitments and assurances (including the wording of the title), but would provide for an economic planning mechanism of some sort in the Executive and legislative branches, and for a moderate program of public works."[3]

While most of the people who testified about the original bill were largely supportive of its goals, there were dissenting voices who thought it dangerously neglected the issue of price stability. Among them was Harvard University economist Gottfried Haberler, who stated:

"It will be essential to prevent partial, localized unemployment from spreading depression to other fields. This can be done by supporting aggregate expenditure if it is necessary; but it does not follow that unemployment can be eradicated by simply spending more until full employment is reached. Long before that point is reached, inflationary price rises would be produced. If it were possible to shift labor and other resources easily and quickly from excess areas to the points where scarcities exist, we would not need to worry. But experience teaches that such shifts cannot always be made sufficiently fast".[4]

Similarly, economist Walter A. Morton of the University of Wisconsin argued, "One of the defects of this bill, in my opinion, is its failure to prescribe a price policy." He elaborated:

"Now I recognize that it is not possible to legislate regarding any particular price, nor regarding any price level, but I do think it is both necessary and desirable to state that it is the policy of the United States to prevent inflation of prices; to maintain a stable level of wholesale prices, and a stable cost of living; provided, however, that such stability shall not preclude a secular downward movement of prices and the cost of living as industrial efficiency increases".[5]

During the 25 years immediately following the passage of the 1946 Act, the American economy generally performed quite well. While there was significant inflation in the last half of the 1940s, annual inflation rates typically ranged from 1 percent to 5 percent during the rest of this period. The labor market also performed quite well, with annual unemployment rates trending around 5 percent. But both inflation and unemployment began to rise in the early 1970s, bringing about a period of "stagflation." Not surprisingly, worsening economic conditions prompted both the president and Congress to act.

President Ford delivered his famous "Whip Inflation Now" (WIN) speech on October 8, 1974, during which he enumerated 10 proposals. His fourth proposal captured the widespread desire to address both inflation and unemployment simultaneously, albeit in a way that was unlikely to prove efficacious and thus demonstrating the difficulty of the problem:

We need more capital. We cannot "eat up our seed corn." Our free enterprise system depends on orderly capital markets through which the savings of our people become productively used. Today, our capital markets are in total disarray. We must restore their vitality. Prudent monetary restraint is essential.

You and the American people should know, however, that I have personally been assured by the Chairman of the independent Federal Reserve Board that the supply of money and credit will expand sufficiently to meet the needs of our economy and that in no event will a credit crunch occur.[6]

Meanwhile, in early 1975, Congress adopted Resolution 133 instructing the Federal Reserve to, among other things:

maintain long run growth of the monetary and credit aggregates commensurate with the economy's long run potential to increase production, so as to promote effectively the goals of maximum employment, stable prices, and moderate long term interest rates.[7]

In 1977, Congress amended the Federal Reserve Act to incorporate the provisions of Resolution 133, but only after debating more ambitious proposals. In a 1976 hearing on the Employment Act of 1946, Senator Hubert Humphrey commented, "It is my judgment that that law has, from time to time, been conveniently ignored."[8] He wanted to adopt legislation that would enumerate more explicit employment goals, and if those goals were not met to have the government provide jobs to achieve the target.

Humphrey also wished to give the executive branch a greater role in the execution of monetary policy. The president would submit his recommendations for monetary policy, and the Federal Reserve Board of Governors would have to respond within 15 days to explain any proposed deviation. Neither proposal passed, but Humphrey and his colleague in the House, Augustus Hawkins, continued to push for similar legislation. Humphrey died in January 1978, but later that year, the "Full Employment and Balanced Growth Act," better known as the Humphrey-Hawkins Act, was signed into law by President Carter.[9]

The Humphrey-Hawkins Act contained numerous objectives, some of them relatively vague and perhaps contradictory, but with respect to unemployment and inflation, the objectives were clear. Within five years, unemployment should not exceed 4 per-cent for people 16 years or older, and inflation should be reduced to 3 percent or less, provided that its reduction would not interfere with the employment goal. And by 1988, the inflation rate should be zero, again provided that pursuing this goal would not interfere with the employment goal.[10] Of course, the legislation was not binding in any real sense. Congress could not simply mandate such unemployment and inflation rates; it could set them only as targets. Still, Congress demonstrated, and made more explicit, the idea that the Federal Reserve should work to achieve both employment and inflation goals.

Not long after the Federal Reserve Act was amended and the Humphrey-Hawkins Act was passed, the Federal Reserve came under scrutiny for ignoring one side of its "dual mandate."[11] Under the leadership of Chairman Paul Volcker, the Federal Reserve pursued an aggressive set of policies designed to reduce inflation. While those policies did bring inflation down from more than 13 percent in 1980 to roughly 3 percent in 1983, unemployment rose sharply during that period, from roughly 7 percent to more than 10 percent, the highest in the postwar period up to that point. Volcker defended the Fed's actions in 1981 testimony to the Senate Committee on Banking, Housing, and Urban Affairs:

> I am wholly convinced—and I think I can speak for the whole Board and whole Open Market Committee— that recognizing that that objective for unemployment [4 percent] cannot be reached in the short run—the kinds of policies we are following offer the best prospect of returning the economy in time to a course where we can combine as full employment as we can get with price stability.

> I bring in price stability because we will not be successful, in my opinion, in pursuing a full employment policy unless we take care of the inflation side of the equation while we are doing it. I think that philosophy is actually embodied in the Humphrey-Hawkins Act itself. I don't think that we have the choice in current circumstances—the old tradeoff analysis—of buying full employment with a little more inflation.

> We found out that doesn't work, and we are in an economic situation in which we can't achieve either of those objectives immediately. We have to work toward both of them; we have to deal with inflation. And the Federal Reserve has particular responsibilities in that connection.[12]

Volcker's explanation did not satisfy many members of Congress, who charged the Federal Reserve with ignoring the employment aspect of its dual man-date. In a 1982 hearing before the House Committee on Banking, Finance, and Urban Affairs, Chairman Fernand St. Germain asked Volcker: "And in order to bring inflation down even further in 1982, how many American citizens are going to have to look forward to sacrificing in the form of unemployment?" He went on to argue that "the question, I think, in the minds of most American people today—it seems to be more important to the American people now than the rate of inflation—and that is unemployment."[13]

Similarly, Volcker faced sharp questioning from Rep. Mary Rose Oakar. "I mean I have to lay it on the line, I do not think you are concerned," she stated. "Here you are mandated by the Humphrey-Hawkins Act, which has as its major goal full employment for the country, and you come to this committee and you say you mentally discount unemployment."[14] (This was not quite an accurate representation of Volcker's views. He had originally made a statement attempting to address the effects of the increase in unemployment on growing budget deficits, stating, "When I look at that deficit, I mentally discount the part that is due to the rise in the unemployment rate and the recession." His argument was that fiscal imbalances were likely to persist even if the economy recovered; he did not dismiss the importance of unemployment generally.)

Eventually, the Fed's policies of steadfastly pursuing price stability did contribute to a favorable macroeconomic environment, with the economy growing and unemployment dropping sharply during the mid- to late-1980s. (Inflation remained relatively tame during this period as well, ranging from roughly 2 percent to 5 percent annually, with most years seeing an increase in prices of 3 percent to 4 percent.) As a result of this apparent success, talk of the Fed's responsibility to pursue its dual mandate largely dropped from public discourse until the mid-1990s, when some members of the Federal Open Market Committee (FOMC) called for the Fed to adopt an explicit inflation target. While this policy had been adopted—in writing if not always in practice—by a number of countries, there was skepticism among other members of the FOMC. Their discomfort with the proposal was due, at least in part, to the belief that an explicit inflation target would not give the Fed sufficient discretion to pursue its mandate of achieving maximum employment, or maximum *sustainable* employment, as some people had begun to refer to the Fed's charge.

In particular, Vice Chairman Alan Blinder was op-posed to such a change in Fed policy. At the January 31– February 1, 1995 meeting of the FOMC, he stated:

As usual, let me defend the status quo. We have a dual objective in the Federal Reserve Act now. I think it works very well. I think the case that it is broken and needs fixing is extremely thin.... There is no existing evidence—and I can't say this too strongly—that having such targets leads to a superior trade-off. None at all. It is not one of those cases in which the evidence is equivocal. There is nothing that can be cited.[15]

While the idea that the Federal Reserve should pursue a "dual objective"—"dual mandate," as Blinder and many in the media soon began to call it—had been around for decades, the term itself did not emerge in common parlance until 1995. Since then, its usage has become widespread among policymakers and journalists. However, it was not until recently that the FOMC addressed employment explicitly in its policy statement. Instead, the FOMC preferred to mention sustainable economic growth and price stability. As Daniel L. Thornton of the Federal Reserve Bank of St. Louis has written:

"..until the September 21, 2010, meeting, there was no reference to the objective of maximum employment elsewhere in the policy directive or in the FOMC's statement." The September statement read, "Measures of underlying inflation are currently at levels somewhat below those the Committee judges most consistent, over the longer run, with its mandate to promote *maximum employment* and price stability" [italics added]. Reference to the objective of maximum employment was more prominent in both the November 2–3, 2010, policy directive and the FOMC's policy statement. Both included the statement, "Consistent with its statutory mandate, the Committee seeks to foster maximum employment and price stability. Currently, the unemployment rate is elevated, and measures of underlying inflation are somewhat low, relative to levels that the Committee judges to be consistent, over the longer run, with its dual mandate.[16]

The FOMC has continued to mention its statutory requirement to seek maximum employment and price stability in subsequent statements. Why the re-cent acknowledgment of the dual mandate in public statements? Any answer to that question is speculative. As Thornton notes:

It is not clear whether the direct reference to the objective of maximum sustainable employment reflects a change in the FOMC's belief regarding the extent to which its actions can affect employment or merely reflects a desire to explicitly recognize its mandate, perhaps motivated by the fact that the unemployment rate remains unacceptably high. In this regard, it is interesting to note that the unemployment rate was 8 percent or higher from November 1981 to January

1984 without a significant change in the wording of the FOMC's policy directive.

During its nearly 100-year history, the Federal Reserve has evolved considerably regarding both the scope of its duties and the actions it has taken to meet them. Prominent during most of its existence, though, has been the idea that it is responsible for both securing the value of the nation's currency as well as promoting employment. At times, public sentiment has seemed to favor one objective over the other, and currently most Americans, understandably, seem more concerned about the high rate of unemployment than inflation. To be sure, unemployment is a significant problem—one that affects millions of struggling American families— and the Fed must continue to be mindful of unemployment when making policy. Toward that end, many economists have argued that, in the long run, the most effective means by which the Fed can help people get back to work is to ensure that prices remain stable, so that businesses can make rational, foresighted decisions that would produce economic growth and a healthier labor market. This remains a topic of much discussion and debate among economists and policymakers. In that regard, the "dual mandate" is far from a historical matter, though why the Fed was given that charge and how it has responded to it in the past perhaps will shed light on proposals to address current macroeconomic problems. ∎

Aaron Steelman is director of publications in the Research Department at the Federal Reserve Bank of Richmond.

Endnotes

1 Quoted in Stephen Kemp Bailey, Congress Makes a Law: The Story Behind the Employment Act of 1946, New York: Columbia University Press, 1950, p. 228.

2 Quoted in Bailey, p. 243.

3 Bailey, p. 165.

4 Letter from Gottfried Haberler to Senator Robert F. Wagner, chairman of the Banking and Currency Committee, May 18, 1945.

5 Letter from Walter A. Morton to Senator Robert F. Wagner, chairman of the Banking and Currency Committee, May 7, 1945.

6 "Whip Inflation Now," Address by President Gerald R. Ford to the U.S. Congress, October 8, 1974.

7 Quoted in Allan H. Meltzer, A History of the Federal Reserve: Volume 2, Book 2, 1970–1986, Chicago: University of Chicago Press, 2009, p. 986.

8 Quoted in Meltzer, p. 987.

9 In a 1986 paper, G.J. Santoni, then of the Federal Reserve Bank of St. Louis, argued that the more ambitious measures of the Humphrey-Hawkins Act were stripped away, as they were from the 1945 bill that became the Employment Act of 1946. He wrote: "The Humphrey-Hawkins Bill of 1976 attempted to revive the

main provisions of the 1945 bill. Congress, however, had become no more sympathetic in the intervening 30 years. As in 1946, they extracted the legislation's teeth before approving it and created an 'unworkable monster' by loading the bill with an agglomeration of conflicting policy statements." See G.J. Santoni, "The Employment Act of 1946: Some History Notes," Federal Reserve Bank of St. Louis Review, Nov. 1986, p. 15.

10 "Full Employment and Balanced Growth Act of 1978," Public Law 95523, October 27, 1978, pp. 8–9.

11 Although the 1977 amendment to the Federal Reserve Act instructed the Fed to pursue three goals— maximum employment, stable prices, and moderate long-term interest rates—the third goal is rarely discussed. In a 2007 speech, former Federal Reserve Governor Frederic S. Mishkin succinctly described the reason for its omission: "Because long-term interest rates can remain low only in a stable macroeconomic environment, these goals are often referred to as the dual mandate; that is, the Federal Reserve seeks to promote the coequal objectives of maximum employment and price stability." See Frederic S. Mishkin, "Monetary Policy and the Dual Mandate," address at Bridgewater College, Bridgewater, Va., April 10, 2007.

12 Federal Reserve Chairman Paul Volcker, "Federal Reserve's First Monetary Policy Report for 1981," Hearings before the U.S. Senate Committee on Banking, Housing, and Urban Affairs, February 25 and March 4, 1981, U.S. Government Printing Office, p. 28.

13 Rep. Fernand St. Germain, "Conduct of Monetary Policy," Hearings before the U.S. House of Representatives Committee on Banking, Finance, and Urban Af-

fairs, February 10 and March 30, 1982, U.S. Government Printing Office, p. 53. Page 6

14 Rep. Mary Rose Oakar, "Conduct of Monetary Policy," Hearings before the U.S. House of Representatives Committee on Banking, Finance, and Urban Affairs, February 10 and March 30, 1982, U.S. Government Printing Office, p. 84.

15 Transcript of the meeting of the Federal Open Market Committee, January 31–February 1, 1995, p. 52.

16 Daniel L. Thornton, "What Does the Change in the FOMC's Statement of Objectives Mean?" Federal Reserve Bank of St. Louis Economic Synopses, 2011, No. 1, p. 2.

-Appendix G-
A One Dollar Bracket Income Tax Scheme

Tax brackets have been used historically, imposing a certain rate on a range of incomes called "the bracket." This is a rather cumbersome way to impose taxes leading to problems such as incomes creeping from one bracket to another. There is general agreement that taxes should be imposed progressively, the rate increasing as income rises. It is difficult to implement this fairly with brackets when an individual at the lower end of the bracket pays the same rate as an individual with a higher income at the top of the bracket.

An interactive program has been developed to demonstrate the "One Dollar" tax bracket scheme. Using five "income level, tax rate" points, the program produces a smooth, continuous and progressive tax rate function. For any level of income the rate at one dollar higher will be a higher tax rate and at one dollar lower will be less. The continuous tax rate function is enabled from the five spot values (more or less than five spot values could be used) by imposing the same tax rate on all incomes at the same level. A person earning 120,000.00 per year would have his first 20,000.00 of income taxed at the same rate as a person earning only 20,000 per year. The fifth point is considered the maximum tax rate and is applied to all incomes greater than that specified in the fifth point. Thus, the actual tax rate is always less than the spot values because it includes the lower rates as well as the current spot rate. At high incomes the rate approaches the rate specified In the fifth point asymptotically. It sounds complicated but it is implemented in just a few lines of computer code!

When the program is started a default set of values for the tax function are loaded and the spot values(red), tax rate(blue) and after tax income(green) curves are shown. The values in the tax model can be changed and new curves and data can be shown using the program controls. New tax models can be saved and accessed later with the program controls.

The program also has income distribution data published by: U.S. Census Bureau, Current Population Survey, 2016 Annual Social and Economic Supplement. Published in 2016, the data is from 2015 income statistics. The Census Bureau's data is shown separately for each gender. The data in the program is from integration of the two sets. The data is coarse and rough. An analytical model was developed approximating the income distribution for 2015 and it is used in the program to calculate tax redemption for any model as a percentage of GNI, Gross National Income.

When a tax calculation is run for a model the results and model data are saved and can be accessed with program controls. Up to twenty six runs can be saved as a group by transferring the data to Windows Notepad using program controls.

When the program is started graphic data is shown in the center, control buttons and data displayed at the top and options plus the default tax model data with a text box to edit the model at the bottom. Each of the controls show usage tips when the mouse lingers over the control, making its use very obvious. The options on the bottom, far right allow selection of a "Full Scale" or "Magnified" view of the data. The "Full Scale" option plots data from zero to 4.2 million dollars income per year. The "Magnified" option plots data from zero to

$500,000 per year.

The income distribution data, both actual and the model, are best viewed with the "Magnified" option because of the preponderance of income at the lower levels between zero and $100,000.00 per year.

With the "View Tax" button at the top both tabular data and graphical data is displayed of tax redemption, income distribution and the final result of tax redemption as a percent of Gross National Income or GNI.

The main window of the program is shown on the following page.

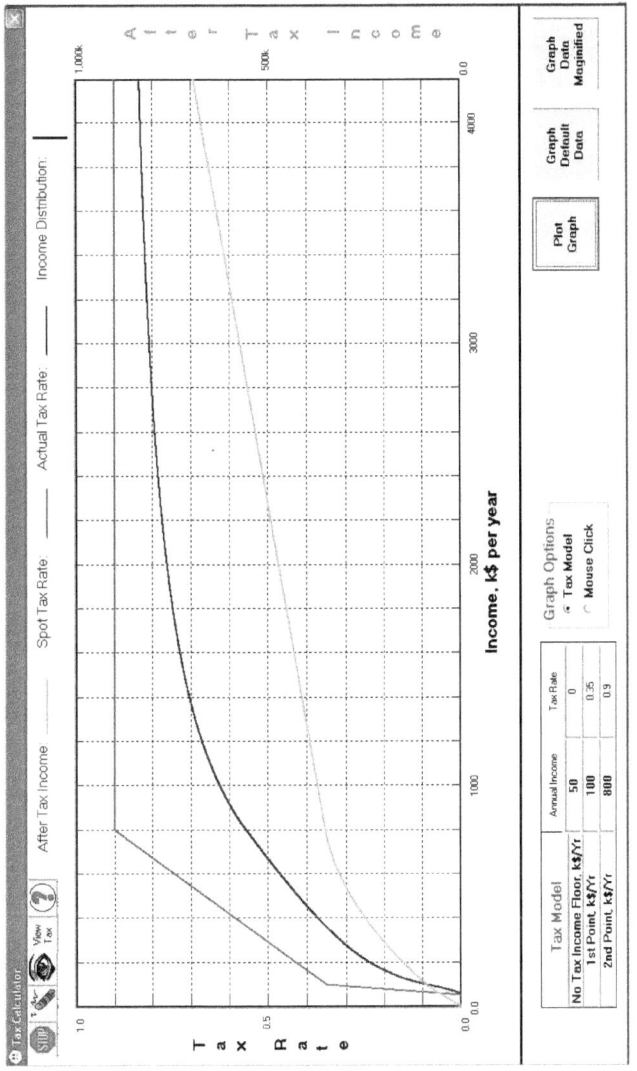

Appendix H
Famous Quotes about Banking

(Taken from: http://www.themoneymasters.com/)

"If the American people ever allow private banks to control the issue of their currency, first by inflation, then by deflation, the banks...will deprive the people of all property until their children wake-up homeless on the continent their fathers conquered.... The issuing power should be taken from the banks and restored to the people, to whom it properly belongs." – **Thomas Jefferson** in the debate over the Re-charter of the Bank Bill (1809)

"The Government should create, issue, and circulate all the currency and credits needed to satisfy the spending power of the Government and the buying power of consumers. By the adoption of these principles, the taxpayers will be saved immense sums of interest. Money will cease to be master and become the servant of humanity." - **Abraham Lincoln**

"Issue of currency should be lodged with the government and be protected from domination by Wall Street. We are opposed to...provisions [which] would place our currency and credit system in private hands." – **Theodore Roosevelt**

"When a government is dependent upon bankers for money, they and not the leaders of the government control the situation, since the hand that gives is above the hand that takes... Money has no motherland; financiers are without patriotism and without decency; their sole object is gain." – **Napoleon Bonaparte**, Emperor of France, 1815

"The death of Lincoln was a disaster for Christendom. There was no man in the United States great enough to wear his boots and the bankers went anew to grab the riches. I fear that foreign bankers with their craftiness and tortuous tricks will entirely control the exuberant riches of America and use it to systematically corrupt civilization." **Otto von Bismark** (1815-1898), German Chancellor, after the Lincoln assassination

"Money plays the largest part in determining the course of history." **Karl Marx** writing in the Communist Manifesto (1848).

"That this House considers that the continued issue of all the means of exchange – be they coin, banknotes or credit, largely passed on by cheques – by private firms as an interest-bearing debt against the public should cease forthwith; that the Sovereign power and duty of issuing money in all forms should be returned to the Crown, then to be put into circulation free of all debt and interest obligations…" **Captain Henry Kerby MP**, in an Early Day Motion tabled in 1964.

"Banks lend by creating credit. They create the means of payment out of nothing. " **Ralph M Hawtry**, former Secretary to the Treasury.

"… our whole monetary system is dishonest, as it is debt-based… We did not vote for it. It grew upon us gradually but markedly since 1971 when the commodity-based system was abandoned." **The Earl of Caithness**, in a speech to the House of Lords, 1997.

"The bank hath benefit of interest on all moneys which it creates out of nothing." **William Paterson**, founder of the Bank of England in 1694, then a privately owned bank

"Let me issue and control a nation's money and I care not who writes the laws." **Mayer Amschel Rothschild** (1744-1812), founder of the House of Rothschild.

"The few who understand the system will either be so interested in its profits or be so dependent upon its favors that there will be no opposition from that class, while on the other hand, the great body of people, mentally incapable of comprehending the tremendous advantage that capital derives from the system, will bear its burdens without complaint, and perhaps without even suspecting that the system is inimical to their interests." The **Rothschild brothers of London** writing to associates in New York, 1863.

"I am afraid the ordinary citizen will not like to be told that the banks can and do create money. And they who control the credit of the nation direct the policy of Governments and hold in the hollow of their hand the destiny of the people." **Reginald McKenna**, as Chairman of the Midland Bank, addressing stockholders in 1924.

"The banks do create money. They have been doing it for a long time, but they didn't realize it, and they did not admit it. Very few did. You will find it in all sorts of documents, financial textbooks, etc. But in the intervening years, and we must be perfectly frank about these things, there has been a development of thought, until today I doubt very much whether you would get many prominent bankers to attempt to deny that banks create it." **H W White**, Chairman of the Associated Banks of New Zealand, to the New Zealand Monetary Commission, 1955.

"Money is a new form of slavery, and distinguishable from the old simply by the fact that it is impersonal – that there is no human relation between master and slave." **Leo Tolstoy**, Russian writer.

"It is well enough that people of the nation do not understand our banking and money system, for if they did, I believe there would be a revolution before tomorrow morning." **Henry Ford**, founder of the Ford Motor Company.

"The modern banking system manufactures money out of nothing. The process is, perhaps, the most astounding piece of sleight of hand that was ever invented. Banks can in fact inflate, mint and un-mint the modern ledger entry currency." **Major L L B Angus**.

"The study of money, above all other fields in economics, is one in which complexity is used to disguise truth or to evade truth, not to reveal it. The process by which banks create money is so simple the mind is repelled. With something so important, a deeper mystery seems only decent." **John Kenneth Galbraith** (1908-), former professor of economics at Harvard, writing in 'Money: Whence it came, where it went' (1975).

As **Nicolas Trist** – secretary to President Andrew Jackson – said about the incredibly powerful privately owned Second Bank of the United States, "Independently of its misdeeds, the mere power, — the bare existence of such a power, — is a thing irreconcilable with the nature and spirit of our institutions." (Schlesinger, The Age of Jackson, p.102)

Appendix I
Reconstruction Finance Corporation

James Butkiewicz
University of Delaware

Introduction

The Reconstruction Finance Corporation (RFC) was established during the Hoover administration with the primary objective of providing liquidity to, and restoring confidence in the banking system. The banking system experienced extensive pressure during the economic contraction of 1929-1933. During the contraction period, many banks had to suspend business operations and most of these ul-timately failed. A number of these suspensions occurred during banking panics, when large numbers of depositors rushed to convert their deposits to cash from fear their bank might fail. Since this period was prior to the establishment of federal deposit insurance, bank depositors lost part or all of their deposits when their bank failed.

During its first thirteen months of operation, the RFC's primary activity was to make loans to banks and financial institutions. During President Roosevelt's New Deal, the RFC's powers were expanded significantly. At various times, the RFC purchased bank preferred stock, made loans to assist agriculture, housing, exports, business, governments, and for disaster relief, and even purchased gold at the President's direction in order to change the market price of gold. The scope of RFC activities was expanded further immediately before and during World War II. The RFC established or purchased, and funded, eight corporations that made important contributions to the war effort. After the war, the RFC's activities were limited primarily to making loans to business. RFC lending ended in 1953, and the corporation ceased operations in 1957, when all remaining assets were transferred to other government agencies.

The Genesis of the Reconstruction Finance Corporation

The difficulties experienced by the American banking system were one of the defining characteristics of the Great Contraction of 1929-1933. During this period, the American banking system was comprised of a very large number of banks. At the end of December 1929, there were 24,633 banks in the United States. The vast majority of these banks were small, serving small towns and rural communities. These small banks were particularly susceptible to local economic difficulties, which could result in failure of the bank.

The Federal Reserve and Small Banks

The Federal Reserve System was created in 1913 to address the problem of periodic banking crises. The Fed had the ability to act as a lender of last resort, providing funds to banks during crises. While nationally chartered banks were required to join the Fed, state-chartered banks could join the Fed at their discretion. Most state-chartered banks chose not to join the Federal Reserve System. The majority of the small banks in rural communities were not Fed members. Thus, during crises, these banks were unable to seek assistance from the Fed, and the Fed felt no obligation to engage in a general expansion of credit to assist nonmember banks.

How Banking Panics Develop

At this time there was no federal deposit insurance system, so bank customers generally lost part or all of their deposits when their bank failed. Fear of failure sometimes caused people to panic. In a panic, bank customers attempt to immediately withdraw their funds. While banks hold enough cash for normal operations, they use most of their deposited funds to make loans and purchase interest-earning assets. In a panic, banks are forced to attempt to rapidly convert these assets to cash. Frequently, they are forced to sell assets at a loss to obtain cash quickly, or may be unable to sell assets at all. As losses accumulate, or cash reserves dwindle, a bank becomes unable to pay all depositors, and must suspend operations. During this period, most banks that suspended operations declared bankruptcy. Bank suspensions and failures may incite panic in adjacent communities or regions. This spread of panic, or contagion, can result in a large number of bank failures. Not only do customers lose some or all of their deposits, but also people become wary of banks in general. A widespread withdrawal of bank deposits reduces the amount of money and credit in society. This monetary contraction can contribute to a recession or depression.

Bank failures were a common event throughout the 1920s. In any year, it was normal for several hundred banks to fail. In 1930, the number of failures increased substantially. Failures and contagious panics occurred repeatedly during the contraction years. President Hoover recognized that the banking system required assistance. However, the President also believed that this assistance, like charity, should come from the private sector rather than the government, if at all possible.

The National Credit Corporation

To this end, Hoover encouraged a number of major

banks to form the National Credit Corporation (NCC), to lend money to other banks experiencing difficulties. The NCC was announced on October 13, 1931, and began operations on November 11, 1931. However, the banks in the NCC were not enthusiastic about this endeavor, and made loans very reluctantly, requiring that borrowing banks pledge their best assets as collateral, or security for the loan. Hoover quickly recognized that the NCC would not provide the necessary relief to the troubled banking system.

RFC Approved, January 1932

Eugene Meyer, Governor of the Federal Reserve Board, convinced the President that a public agency was needed to make loans to troubled banks. On December 7, 1931, a bill was introduced to establish the Reconstruction Finance Corporation. The legislation was approved on January 22, 1932, and the RFC opened for business on February 2, 1932.

The original legislation authorized the RFC's existence for a ten-year period. However, Presidential approval was required to operate beyond January

1, 1933, and Congressional approval was required for lending authority to continue beyond January 1, 1934. Subsequent legislation extended the life of the RFC and added many additional responsibilities and authorities.

The RFC was funded through the United States Treasury. The Treasury provided $500 million of capital to the RFC, and the RFC was authorized to borrow an additional $1.5 billion from the Treasury. The Treasury, in turn, sold bonds to the public to fund the RFC. Over time, this borrowing authority was increased many fold. Subsequently, the RFC was authorized to sell securities directly to the public to obtain funds. However, most RFC funding was obtained by borrowing from the Treasury. During its years of existence, the RFC borrowed $51.3 billion from the Treasury, and $3.1 billion from the public.

The RFC During the Hoover Administration
RFC Authorized to Lend to Banks and Others

The original legislation authorized the RFC to make loans to banks and other financial institutions, to railroads, and for crop loans. While the original objective of the RFC was to help banks, railroads were assisted because many banks owned railroad bonds, which had declined in value, because the railroads themselves had suffered from a decline in their business. If railroads recovered, their bonds would increase in value. This increase, or appreciation, of bond prices would improve the financial condition of banks holding these bonds.

Through legislation approved on July 21, 1932, the RFC was authorized to make loans for self-liquidating public works project, and to states to provide relief and work relief to needy and unemployed people. This legislation also required that the RFC report to Congress, on a monthly basis, the identity of all new borrowers of RFC funds.

RFC Undercut by Requirement That It Publish Names of Banks Receiving Loans

From its inception through Franklin Roosevelt's inauguration on March 4, 1933, the RFC primarily made loans to financial institutions. During the first months following the establishment of the RFC, bank failures and currency holdings outside of banks both declined. However, several loans aroused political and public controversy, which was the reason the July 21, 1932 legislation included the provision that the identity of banks receiving RFC loans from this date forward be reported to Congress. The Speaker of the House of Representatives, John Nance Garner, ordered that the identity of the borrowing banks be made public. The publication of the identity of banks receiving RFC loans, which began in August 1932, reduced the effectiveness of RFC lending. Bankers became reluctant to borrow from the RFC, fearing that public revelation of a RFC loan would cause depositors to fear the bank was in danger of failing, and possibly start a panic. Legislation passed in January 1933 required that the RFC publish a list of all loans made from its inception through July 21, 1932, the effective date for the publication of new loan recipients.

RFC, Politics and Bank Failure in February and March 1933

In mid-February 1933, banking difficulties developed in Detroit, Michigan. The RFC was willing to make a loan to the troubled bank, the Union Guardian Trust, to avoid a crisis. The bank was one of Henry Ford's banks, and Ford had deposits of $7 million in this particular bank. Michigan Senator James Couzens demanded that Henry Ford subordinate his deposits in the troubled bank as a condition of the loan. If Ford agreed, he would risk losing all of his deposits before any other depositor lost a penny. Ford and Couzens had once been partners in the automotive business, but had become bitter rivals. Ford refused to agree to Couzens' demand, even though failure to save the bank might start a panic in Detroit. When the negotiations failed, the governor of Michigan declared a statewide bank holiday. In spite of the RFC's willingness to assist the Union Guardian Trust, the crisis could not be averted.

The crisis in Michigan resulted in a spread of panic, first to adjacent states, but ultimately throughout the nation. By the day of Roosevelt's inauguration, March 4, all states had declared bank holidays or had restricted the withdrawal of bank deposits for cash. As one of his first acts as president, on March 5 President Roosevelt announced to the nation that he was declaring a nationwide bank holiday. Almost all financial institutions in the nation were closed for business during the following week. The RFC lending program failed to prevent the worst financial crisis in American history.

Criticisms of the RFC

The effectiveness of RFC lending to March 1933 was limited in several respects. The RFC required banks to pledge assets as collateral for RFC loans. A criticism of the RFC was that it often took a bank's best loan assets as collateral. Thus, the liquidity provided came at a steep price to banks. Also, the publicity of new loan recipients beginning in August 1932, and general controversy surrounding RFC lending probably discouraged banks from borrowing. In September and November 1932, the amount of outstanding RFC loans to banks and trust companies decreased, as repayments exceeded new lending.

The RFC in the New Deal
FDR Sees Advantages in Using the RFC

President Roosevelt inherited the RFC. He and his

colleagues, as well as Congress, found the independence and flexibility of the RFC to be particularly useful. The RFC was an executive agency with the ability to obtain funding through the Treasury outside of the normal legislative process. Thus, the RFC could be used to finance a variety of favored projects and programs without obtaining legislative approval. RFC lending did not count toward budgetary expenditures, so the expansion of the role and influence of the government through the RFC was not reflected in the federal budget.

RFC Given the Authority to Buy Bank Stock

The first task was to stabilize the banking system. On March 9, 1933, the Emergency Banking Act was approved as law. This legislation and a subsequent amendment improved the RFC's ability to assist banks by giving it the authority to purchase bank preferred stock, capital notes and debentures (bonds), and to make loans using bank preferred stock as collateral. While banks were initially reluctant, the RFC encouraged banks to issue preferred stock for it to purchase. This provision of capital funds to banks strengthened the financial position of many banks. Banks could use the new capital funds to expand their lending, and did not have to pledge their best assets as collateral. The RFC purchased $782 million of bank preferred stock from 4,202 individual banks, and $343 million of capital notes and debentures from 2,910 individual bank and trust companies. In sum, the RFC assisted almost 6,800 banks. Most of these purchases occurred in the years 1933 through 1935.

The preferred stock purchase program did have controversial aspects. The RFC officials at times exercised their authority as shareholders to reduce salaries of senior bank officers, and on occasion, insisted upon a change of bank management. However, the infusion of new capital into the banking system, and the establishment of the Federal Deposit Insurance Corporation to insure bank depositors against loss, stabilized the financial system. In the years following 1933, bank failures declined to very low levels.

RFC's Assistance to Farmers

Throughout the New Deal years, the RFC's assistance to farmers was second only to its assistance to bankers. Total RFC lending to agricultural financing institutions totaled $2.5 billion. Over half, $1.6 billion, went to its subsidiary, the Commodity Credit Corporation. The Commodity Credit Corporation was incorporated in Delaware in 1933, and operated by the RFC for six years. In 1939, control of the Commodity Credit Corporation was transferred to the Department of Agriculture, were it remains today.

Commodity Credit Corporation

The agricultural sector was hit particularly hard by depression, drought, and the introduction of the tractor, displacing many small and tenant farmers. The primary New Deal program for farmers was the Agricultural Adjustment Act. Its objective was to reverse the decline of product prices and farm incomes experienced since 1920. The Commodity Credit Corporation contributed to this objective by purchasing selected agricultural products at guaranteed prices, typically above the prevailing market price. Thus, the CCC purchases established a guaranteed minimum price for these farm products.

The RFC also funded the Electric Home and Farm Authority, a program designed to enable low- and moderate- income households to purchase gas and electric appliances. This program would create demand for electricity in rural areas, such as the area served by the new Tennessee Valley Authority. Providing electricity to rural areas was the objective of the Rural Electrification Program.

Decline in Bank Lending Concerns RFC and New Deal Officials

After 1933, bank assets and bank deposits both increased. However, banks changed their asset allocation dramatically during the recovery years. Prior to the depression, banks primarily made loans, and purchased some securities, such as U.S. Treasury securities. During the recovery years, banks primarily purchased securities, which involved less risk. Whether due to concerns over safety, or because potential borrowers had weakened financial positions due to the depression, bank lending did not recover as shown in Table 1 on the following page.

Table 1:

Year	Bank Loans and Investments in Millions of Dollars	Bank Loans in Millions of Dollars	Bank Net Deposits in Millions of Dollars	Loans as a % of Loans and Investments	Loans as a % of Net Deposits
1921	39895	28927	30129	73%	96%
1922	39837	27627	31803	69%	87%
1923	43613	30272	34359	69%	88%
1924	45067	31409	36660	70%	86%
1925	48709	33729	40349	69%	84%
1926	51474	36035	42114	70%	86%
1927	53645	37208	43489	69%	86%
1928	57683	39507	44911	68%	88%
1929	58899	41581	45058	71%	92%
1930	58556	40497	45586	69%	89%
1931	55267	35285	41841	64%	84%
1932	46310	27888	32166	60%	87%
1933	40305	22243	28468	55%	78%
1934	42552	21306	32184	50%	66%
1935	44347	20213	35662	46%	57%
1936	48412	20636	41027	43%	50%
1937	49565	22410	42765	45%	52%
1938	47212	20982	41752	44%	50%
1939	49616	21320	45557	43%	47%
1940	51336	22340	49951	44%	45%

Source: Banking and Monetary Statistics, 1914 –1941.

Net Deposits are total deposits less interbank deposits.

All data for the last business day of June in each year.

The relative decline in bank lending was a major concern for RFC officials and the New Dealers, who felt that lack of lending by banks was hindering economic recovery. The sentiment within the Roosevelt administration was that the problem was banks' unwillingness to lend. They viewed the lending by the Commodity Credit Corporation and the Electric Home and Farm Authority, as well as reports from members of Congress, as evidence that there was unsatisfied business loan demand.

RFC Provides Credit to Business

Due to the failure of bank lending to return to pre-Depression levels, the role of the RFC expanded to include the provision of credit to business. RFC support was deemed as essential for the success of the National Recovery Administration, the New Deal program designed to promote industrial recovery. To support the NRA, legislation passed in 1934 authorized the RFC and the Federal Reserve System to make working capital loans to businesses. However, direct lending to businesses did not become an important RFC activity until 1938, when President Roosevelt encouraged expanding business lending in response to the recession of 1937-38.

RFC Mortgage Company

During the depression, many families and individuals were unable to make their mortgage payments, and had their homes repossessed. Another New Deal goal was to provide more funding for mortgages, to avoid the displacement of homeowners. In June 1934, the National Housing Act provided for the establishment of the Federal Housing Administration (FHA). The FHA would insure mortgage lenders against loss, and FHA mortgages required a smaller percentage down payment than was customary at that time, thus making it easier to purchase a house. In 1935, the RFC Mortgage Company was established to buy and sell FHA-insured mortgages.

RFC and Fannie Mae

Financial institutions were reluctant to purchase FHA mortgages, so in 1938 the President requested that the RFC establish a national mortgage association, the Federal National Mortgage Association, or

Fannie Mae. Fannie Mae was originally funded by the RFC to create a market for FHA and later Veterans Administration (VA) mortgages. The RFC Mortgage Company was absorbed by the RFC in 1947. When the RFC was closed, its remaining mortgage assets were transferred to Fannie Mae. Fannie Mae evolved into a private corporation. During its existence, the RFC provided $1.8 billion of loans and capital to its mortgage subsidiaries.

RFC and Export-Import Bank

President Roosevelt sought to encourage trade with the Soviet Union. To promote this trade, the Export-Import Bank was established in 1934. The RFC provided capital, and later loans to the Ex-Im Bank. Interest in loans to support trade was so strong that a second Ex-Im bank was created to fund trade with other foreign nations a month after the first bank was created. These two banks were merged in 1936, with the authority to make loans to encourage exports in general. The RFC provided $201 million of capital and loans to the Ex-Im Banks.

Other RFC activities during this period included

lending to federal government agencies providing relief from the depression including the Public Works Administration and the Works Progress Administration, disaster loans, and loans to state and local governments.

RFC Pushed Up the Price of Gold, Devalues the Dollar

Evidence of the flexibility afforded through the RFC was President Roosevelt's use of the RFC to affect the market price of gold. The President wanted to reduce the gold value of the dollar from $20.67 per ounce of gold. As the dollar price of gold increased, the dollar exchange rate would fall relative to currencies that had a fixed gold price. A fall in the value of the dollar makes exports cheaper and imports more expensive. In an economy with high levels of unemployment, a decline in imports and increase in exports would increase domestic employment.

The goal of the RFC purchases was to increase the market price of gold. During October 1933 the RFC began purchasing gold at a price of $31.36 per ounce. The price was gradually increased to over

$34 per ounce. The RFC price set a floor for the price of gold. In January 1934, the new official dollar price of gold was fixed at $35.00 per ounce, a 59% devaluation of the dollar.

Twice President Roosevelt instructed Jesse Jones, the president of the RFC, to stop lending, as he intended to close the RFC. The first occasion was in October 1937, and the second was in early 1940. The recession of 1937-38 caused Roosevelt to authorize the resumption of RFC lending in early 1938. The German invasion of France and the Low Countries gave the RFC new life on the second occasion.

The RFC in World War II

In 1940 the scope of RFC activities increased significantly, as the United States began preparing to assist its allies, and for possible direct involvement in the war. The RFC's wartime activities were conducted in cooperation with other government agencies involved in the war effort. For its part, the RFC established seven new corporations, and purchased an existing corporation. The eight RFC wartime subsidiaries are listed below.

RFC Wartime Subsidiaries

Metals Reserve Company
Rubber Reserve Company
Defense Plant Corporation
Defense Supplies Corporation
War Damage Corporation
U.S. Commercial Company
Rubber Development Corporation
Petroleum Reserve Corporation (later War Assets Corporation)
Source: Final Report of the Reconstruction Finance Corporation

Development of Materials Cut Off By the War

The RFC subsidiary corporations assisted the war effort as needed. These corporations were involved in funding the development of synthetic rubber, construction and operation of a tin smelter, and establishment of abaca (Manila hemp) plantations in Central America. Both natural rubber and abaca (used to produce rope products) were produced primarily in south Asia, which came under Japanese control. Thus, these programs encouraged the development of alternative sources of supply of these essential materials. Synthetic rubber, which was not produced in the United States prior to the war, quickly became the primary source of rubber in the post-war years.

Other War-Related Activities

Other war-related activities included financing plant conversion and construction for the production of military and essential goods, to deal and stockpile strategic materials, to purchase materials to reduce the supply available to enemy nations, to administer war damage insurance programs, and to finance construction of oil pipelines from Texas to New Jersey to free tankers for other uses.

During its existence, RFC management made discretionary loans and investments of $38.5 billion, of which $33.3 billion was actually disbursed. Of this total, $20.9 billion was disbursed to the RFC's wartime subsidiaries. From 1941 through 1945, the RFC authorized over $2 billion of loans and investments each year, with a peak of over $6 billion authorized in 1943. The magnitude of RFC lending had increased substantially during the war. Most lending to wartime subsidiaries ended in 1945, and all such lending ended in 1948.

The Final Years of the RFC, 1946-1953

After the war, RFC lending decreased dramatically. In the postwar years, only in 1949 was over $1 billion authorized. Through 1950, most of this lending was directed toward businesses and mortgages. On September 7, 1950, Fannie Mae was transferred to the Housing and Home Finance Agency. During its last three years, almost all RFC loans were to businesses, including loans authorized under the Defense Production Act.

Eisenhower Terminates the RFC

President Eisenhower was inaugurated in 1953, and shortly thereafter legislation was passed terminating the RFC. The original RFC legislation authorized operations for one year of a possible ten-year existence, giving the President the option of extending its operation for a second year without Congressional approval. The RFC survived much longer, continuing to provide credit for both the New Deal and World War II. Now, the RFC would finally be closed.

Small Business Administration

However, there was concern that the end of RFC business loans would hurt small businesses. Thus, the Small Business Administration (SBA) was created in 1953 to continue the program of lending to small businesses, as well as providing training programs for entrepreneurs. The disaster loan program was also transferred to the SBA.

Through legislation passed on July 30, 1953, RFC lending authority ended on September 28, 1953. The RFC continued to collect on its loans and investments through June 30, 1957, at which time all remaining assets were transferred to other government agencies. At the time the liquidation act was passed, the RFC's production of synthetic rubber, tin, and abaca remained in operation. Synthetic rubber operations were sold or leased to private industry. The tin and abaca programs were ultimately transferred to the General Services Administration.

Successors of the RFC

Three government agencies and one private corporation that were related to the RFC continue today. The Small Business Administration was established to continue lending to small businesses. The Commodity Credit Corporation continues to provide assistance to farmers. The Export-Import Bank continues to provide loans to promote exports. Fannie Mae became a private corporation in 1968. Today it is the most important source of mortgage funds in the nation, and has become one of the largest corporations in the country. Its stock is traded on the New York Stock Exchange under the symbol FNM.

Economic Analysis of the RFC
Role of a Lender of Last Resort

The American central bank, the Federal Reserve System, was created to be a lender of last resort. A lender of last resort exists to provide liquidity to banks during crises. The famous British central banker, Walter Bagehot, advised, "...in a panic the holders of the ultimate Bank reserve (whether one bank or many) should lend to all that bring good securities quickly, freely, and readily. By that policy they allay a panic..."

However, the Fed was not an effective lender of last resort during the depression years. Many of the banks experiencing problems during the depression years were not members of the Federal Reserve System, and thus could not borrow from the Fed. The Fed was reluctant to assist troubled banks, and banks also feared that borrowing from the Fed might weaken depositors' confidence.

President Hoover hoped to restore stability and confidence in the banking system by creating the Reconstruction Finance Corporation. The RFC made collateralized loans to banks. Many scholars argue that initially RFC lending did provide relief. These observations are based on the decline in bank suspensions and public currency holdings in the months immediately following the creation of the

RFC in February 1932. These data are presented in Table 2. Bank suspensions occur when banks cannot open for normal business operations due to financial problems. Most bank suspensions ended in failure of the bank. Currency held by the public can be an indicator of public confidence in banks. As confidence declines, members of the public convert deposits to currency, and vice versa.

Table 2:

1932	Currency, M$	Bank Suspensions
January	4896	342
February	4824	119
March	4743	45
April	4751	74
May	4746	82
June	4959	151
July	5048	132
August	4988	85
September	4941	67
October	4863	102
November	4842	93
December	4830	161

Data sources: Currency – Friedman and Schwartz
(1963)
Bank suspensions Board of Governors (1937)

The banking situation deteriorated in June 1932
when a crisis developed in and around Chicago.
Both Friedman and Schwartz (1963) and Jones
(1951) assert that an RFC loan to a key bank helped
to end the crisis, even though the bank subsequently failed.

The Debate over the Impact of the RFC

Two studies of RFC lending have come to differing
conclusions. Butkiewicz (1995) examines the effect
of RFC lending on bank suspensions and finds that
lending reduced suspensions in the months prior to
publication of the identities of loan recipients. He
further argues that publication of the identities of
banks receiving loans discouraged banks from borrowing. As noted above, RFC loans to banks declined in two months after publication began. Mason (2001) examines the impact of lending on a
sample of Illinois banks and finds that those receiv-

ing RFC loans were increasingly likely to fail. Thus, the limited evidence provided from scholarly studies provides conflicting results about the impact of RFC lending.

Critics of RFC lending to banks argue that the RFC took the banks' best assets as collateral, thereby reducing bank liquidity. Also, RFC lending requirements were initially very stringent. After the financial collapse in March 1933, the RFC was authorized to provide banks with capital through preferred stock and bond purchases. This change, along with the creation of the Federal Deposit Insurance System, stabilized the banking system.

Economic and Noneconomic Rationales for an Agency Like the RFC

Beginning 1933, the RFC became more directly involved in the allocation of credit throughout the economy. There are several economic reasons why a government agency might actively participate in the allocation of liquid capital funds. These are market failure, externalities, and noneconomic reasons.

A market failure occurs if private markets fail to allocate resources efficiently. For example, small business owners complain that markets do not provide enough loans at reasonable interest rates, a so-called "credit gap". However, small business loans are riskier than loans to large corporations. Higher interest rates compensate for the greater risk involved in lending to small businesses. Thus, the case for a market failure is not compelling. However, small business loans remain politically popular.

An externality exists when the benefits to society are greater than the benefits to the individuals involved. For example, loans to troubled banks may prevent a financial crisis. Purchases of bank capital may also help stabilize the financial system. Prevention of financial crises and the possibility of a recession or depression provide benefits to society beyond the benefits to bank depositors and shareholders. Similarly, encouraging home ownership may create a more stable society. This argument is often used to justify government provision of funds to the mortgage market.

While wars are often fought over economic issues, and wars have economic consequences, a nation may become involved in a war for noneconomic reasons. Thus, the RFC wartime programs were motivated by political reasons, as much or more than economic reasons.

The RFC was a federal credit agency. The first federal credit agency was established in 1917. However, federal credit programs were relatively limited until the advent of the RFC. Many RFC lending programs were targeted to help specific sectors of the economy. A number of these activities were controversial, as are some federal credit programs today. Three important government agencies and one private corporation that descended from the RFC still operate today. All have important effects on the allocation of credit in our economy.

Criticisms of Governmental Credit Programs

Critics of federal credit programs cite several problems. One is that these programs subsidize certain activities, which may result in overproduction and misallocation of resources. For example, small businesses can obtain funds through the SBA at lower interest rates than are available through banks. This interest rate differential is a subsidy to small business borrowers. Crop loans and price supports result in overproduction of agricultural products. In general, federal credit programs reallocate capital resources to favored activities.

Finally, federal credit programs, including the RFC, are not funded as part of the normal budget process. They obtain funds through the Treasury, or their own borrowings are assumed to have the guarantee of the federal government. Thus, their borrowing is based on the creditworthiness of the federal government, not their own activities. These "off-budget" activities increase the scope of federal involvement in the economy while avoiding the normal budgetary decisions of the President and Congress. Also, these lending programs involve risk. Default on a significant number of these loans might require the federal government to bail out the affected agency. Taxpayers would bear the cost of a bailout.

Any analysis of market failures, externalities, or federal programs should involve a comparison of costs and benefits. However, precise measurement of costs and benefits in these cases is often difficult. Supporters value the benefits very highly, while opponents argue that the costs are excessive.

Conclusion

The RFC was created to assist banks during the Great Depression. It experienced some, albeit limited, success in this activity. However, the RFC's authority to borrow directly from the Treasury outside the normal budget process proved very attractive to President Roosevelt and his advisors. Throughout the New Deal, the RFC was used to finance a vast array of favored activities. During World War II, RFC lending to its subsidiary corporations was an essential component of the war effort. It was the largest and most important federal credit program of its time. Even after the RFC was closed, some of its lending activities have continued through agencies and corporations that were first established or funded by the RFC. These descendent organizations, especially Fannie Mae, play a very important role in the allocation of credit in the American economy. The legacy of the RFC continues, long after it ceased to exist.

Data Sources

Banking data are from Banking and Monetary Statistics, 1914-1941, Board of Governors of the Federal Reserve System, 1943.

RFC data are from Final Report on the Reconstruction Finance Corporation, Secretary of the Treasury, 1959.

Currency data are from The Monetary History of the United States, 1867-1960, Friedman and Schwartz, 1963.

Bank suspension data are from Federal Reserve Bulletin, Board of Governors, September 1937.

References
Bagehot, Walter. Lombard Street: A Description of the Money Market. New York: Scribner, Armstrong & Co., 1873.

Board of Governors of the Federal Reserve System. Banking and Monetary Statistics, 1914-1941. Washington, DC, 1943.

Board of Governors of the Federal Reserve System. Federal Reserve Bulletin. September 1937.

Bremer, Cornelius D. American Bank Failures. New York: AMS Press, 1968.

Butkiewicz, James L. "The Impact of a Lender of Last Resort

during the Great Depression: The Case of the Reconstruction Finance Corporation." Explorations in Economic History 32, no. 2 (1995): 197-216.

Butkiewicz, James L. "The Reconstruction Finance Corporation, the Gold Standard, and the Banking Panic of 1933." Southern Economic Journal 66, no. 2 (1999): 271-93.

Chandler, Lester V. America's Greatest Depression, 1929-1941. New York: Harper and Row, 1970.

Friedman, Milton, and Anna J. Schwartz. The Monetary History of the United States, 1867-1960. Princeton, NJ: Princeton University Press, 1963.

Jones, Jesse H. Fifty Billion Dollars: My Thirteen Years with the RFC, 1932-1945. New York: Macmillan Co., 1951.

Keehn, Richard H., and Gene Smiley. "U.S. Bank Failures, 1932-1933: A Provisional Analysis." Essays in Economic and Business History 6 (1988): 136-56.

Keehn, Richard H., and Gene Smiley. "U.S. Bank Failures, 1932-33: Additional Evidence on Regional Patterns, Timing, and the Role of the Reconstruction Finance Corporation." Essays in Economic and Business History 11 (1993): 131-45.

Kennedy, Susan E. The Banking Crisis of 1933. Lexington, KY: University of Kentucky Press, 1973.

Mason, Joseph R. "Do Lender of Last Resort Policies Matter? The Effects of Reconstruction Finance Corporation Assistance to Banks During the Great Depression." Journal of Financial Services Research 20, no 1. (2001): 77-95.

Nadler, Marcus, and Jules L. Bogen. The Banking Crisis: The End of an Epoch. New York, NY: Arno Press, 1980.

Olson, James S. Herbert Hoover and the Reconstruction Finance Corporation. Ames, IA: Iowa State University Press, 1977.

Olson, James S. Saving Capitalism: The Reconstruction Finance Corporation in the New Deal, 1933-1940. Princeton, NJ: Princeton University Press, 1988.

Saulnier, R. J., Harold G. Halcrow, and Neil H. Jacoby. Federal Lending and Loan Insurance. Princeton, NJ: Princeton University Press, 1958.

Schlesinger, Jr., Arthur M. The Age of Roosevelt: The Coming of the New Deal. Cambridge, MA: Riverside Press, 1957.

Secretary of the Treasury, Final Report on the Reconstruction Finance Corporation. Washington, DC: United States Government Printing Office, 1959.

Sprinkel, Beryl Wayne. "Economic Consequences of the Operations of the Reconstruction Finance Corporation." Journal of Business of the University of Chicago 25, no. 4 (1952): 211-24.

Sullivan, L. Prelude to Panic: The Story of the Bank Holiday. Washington, DC: Statesman Press, 1936.

Trescott, Paul B. "Bank Failures, Interest Rates, and the Great Currency Outflow in the United States, 1929-1933." Research in Economic History 11 (1988): 49-80.

Upham, Cyril B., and Edwin Lamke. Closed and Distressed Banks: A Study in Public Administration. Washington, DC: Brookings Institution, 1934.

Wicker, Elmus. The Banking Panics of the Great Depression. Cambridge: Cambridge University Press, 1996.

Web Links

Commodity Credit Corporation:
http://www.fsa.usda.gov/pas/publications/facts/html/ccc99.htm
Ex-Im Bank: http://www.exim.gov/history.html

Fannie Mae: http://www.fanniemae.com/company/history.html

Small Business Administration:
http://www.sba.gov/aboutsba/sbahistory.doc

Citation: Butkiewicz, James. "Reconstruction Finance Corporation". EH.Net Encyclopedia, edited by Robert Whaples. July 19, 2002. URL http://eh.net/encyclopedia/reconstruction-finance-corporation/

Appendix J

REVIVE LINCOLN'S MONETARY POLICY: AN OPEN LETTER TO PRESIDENT OBAMA

Ellen Brown, April 8th, 2009
http://www.webofdebt.com/articles/lincoln_obama.php

Dear President Obama:

The world was transfixed on that remarkable day in January when, to poetry, song, and dance, you gazed upon Abraham Lincoln's likeness at the Lincoln Memorial and searched for wisdom to navigate these difficult times. Indeed, you have so many things in common with that venerable President that one might imagine you were his reincarnation in different dress. You are both thin and wiry, brilliant speakers, appearing on the national stage at pivotal times. Fertile imaginations could envision you coming back dressed in that African heritage you freed, to help heal the great scar of slavery and prove once and for all the proposition that all men are created equal and can achieve great things if given a fighting chance.

As Wordsworth said, however, our birth is but a sleep and a forgetting; and if that is true, you may have forgotten a more subtle form of slavery from which Lincoln tried less successfully to free his countrymen. You may have forgotten it because it has been omitted from our popular history books, leaving Americans ill-equipped to interpret the lessons of our own past.

This letter is therefore meant to remind you. President Obama, we are now met on another battlefield of that same economic war that visited Lincoln and the Founding Fathers before him. For you to finish the work Lincoln started would be a poetic triumph no American could miss. The fate of our economy and the nation itself may depend on how well you understand Lincoln's monetary breakthrough, the most far-reaching "economic stimulus plan" ever implemented by a U.S. President. You can solve our economic crisis quickly and permanently, by implementing the same economic solution that allowed Lincoln to win the Civil War and thus save the Union from foreign economic masters.

Lincoln's Monetary Breakthrough
The bankers had Lincoln's government over a barrel, just as Wall Street has Congress in its vice-like grip today. The North needed money to fund a war, and the bankers were willing to lend it only under circumstances that amounted to extortion, involving staggering interest rates of 24 to 36 percent.
Lincoln saw that this would bankrupt the North and asked a trusted colleague to research the matter and find a solution. In what may be the best piece of advice ever given to a sitting President, Colonel Dick Taylor of Illinois reported back that the Union had the power under the Constitution to solve its financing problem by printing its money as a sovereign government. Taylor said:

"Just get Congress to pass a bill authorizing the printing of full legal tender treasury notes . . . and pay your soldiers with them and go ahead and win your war with them also. If you make them full legal tender . . . they will have the full sanction of the government and be just as good as any money; as Congress is given that express right by the Constitution."

The Greenbacks actually were just as good as the bankers' banknotes. Both were created on a printing press, but the banknotes had the veneer of legitimacy because they were "backed" by gold. The catch was that this backing was based on "fractional reserves," meaning the bankers held only a small fraction of the gold necessary to support all the loans represented by their banknotes. The "fractional reserve" ruse is still used today to create the impression that bankers are lending something other than mere debt created with accounting entries on their books.1 Lincoln took Col. Taylor's advice and funded the war by printing paper notes backed by the credit of the government. These legal-tender U.S. Notes or "Greenbacks" represented receipts for labor and goods delivered to the United States. They were paid to soldiers and suppliers and were tradable for goods and services of a value equivalent to their service to the community. The Greenbacks aided the Union not only in winning the war but in funding a period of unprecedented economic expansion. Lincoln's government created the greatest industrial giant the world had yet seen. The steel industry was launched, a continental railroad system was created, a new era of farm machinery and cheap tools was promoted, free higher education was established, government support was provided to all branches of science, the Bureau of Mines was organized, and labor productivity was increased by 50 to 75 percent. The Greenback was not the only currency used to fund these achievements; but they could not have been accomplished without it, and they could not have been accomplished on money borrowed at the usurious rates the bankers were attempting to extort from the North.

Lincoln succeeded in restoring the government's power to issue the national currency, but his revolutionary monetary policy was opposed by powerful forces. The threat to established interests was captured in an editorial of unknown authorship, said to have been published in The London Times in 1865:

"If that mischievous financial policy which had its origin in the North American Republic during the late war in that country, should become indurated down to a fixture, then that Government will furnish its own money without cost. It will pay off its debts and be without debt. It will become prosperous beyond precedent in the history of the civilized governments of the world. The brains and wealth of all countries will go to North America. That government must be destroyed or it will destroy every monarchy on the globe."

Lincoln was assassinated in 1865. According to historian W. Cleon Skousen:

"Right after the Civil War there was considerable talk about reviving Lincoln's brief experiment with the Constitutional monetary system. Had not the European money-trust intervened, it would have no doubt become an established institution."

The institution that became established instead was the Federal Reserve, a privately-owned central bank given the power in 1913 to print Federal Reserve Notes (or dollar bills) and lend them to the government. The government was submerged in a debt that has grown exponentially since, until it is now an unrepayable $11 trillion. For nearly a century, Lincoln's statue at the Lincoln Memorial has gazed out pensively across the reflecting pool toward the Federal Reserve building, as if pondering what the bankers had wrought since his death and how to remedy it.

Building on a Successful Tradition

Lincoln did not invent government-issued paper money. Rather, he restored a brilliant innovation of the American colonists. According to Benjamin Franklin, it was the colonists' home-grown paper "scrip" that was responsible for the remarkable abundance in the colonies at a time when England was suffering from the ravages of the Industrial Revolution. Like with Lincoln's Greenbacks, this prosperity posed a threat to the control of the British Crown and the emerging network of private British banks, prompting the King to ban the colonists' paper money and require the payment of taxes in gold. According to Franklin and several other historians of the period, it was these onerous demands by the Crown, and the corresponding collapse of the colonists' paper money supply, that actually sparked the

Revolutionary War.2

The colonists won the war but ultimately lost the money power to a private banking cartel, one that issued another form of paper money called "banknotes." Today the bankers' debt-based money has come to dominate most of the economies of the world; but there are a number of historical examples of the successful funding of economic development in other countries simply with government-issued credit. In Australia and New Zealand in the 1930s, the Depression conditions suffered elsewhere were avoided by drawing on a national credit card issued by publicly-owned central banks. The governments of the island states of Guernsey and Jersey created thriving economies that carried no federal debt, just by issuing their own debt-free public currencies. China has also funded impressive internal development through a system of state-owned banks.

Here in the United States, the state of North Dakota has a wholly state-owned bank that creates credit on its books just as private banks do. This credit is used to serve the needs of the community, and the interest on loans is returned to the government. Not coincidentally, North Dakota has a $1.2 billion budget surplus at a time when 46 of 50 states are insolvent, an impressive achievement for a state of isolated farmers battling challenging weather.3 The North Dakota prototype could be copied not only in every U.S. state but at the federal level.

The Perennial Inflation Question

The objection invariably raised to government-issued currency or credit is that it would create dangerous hyperinflation. However, in none of these models has that proven to be true. Price inflation results either when the supply of money goes up but the supply of goods doesn't, or when speculators devalue currencies by massive short selling, as in those cases of Latin American hyperinflation when printing-press money was used to pay off foreign debt.

When new money is used to produce new goods and services, price inflation does not result because supply and demand rise together. Prices did increase during the American Civil War, but this was attributed to the scarcity of goods common in wartime rather than to the Greenback itself. War produces weapons rather than consumer goods.

Today, with trillions of dollars being committed for bailouts and stimulus plans, another objection to Lincoln's solution is likely to be, "The U.S. government is already printing its own money – and lots of it." This, however, is a misconception. What the government prints are bonds – its I.O.U.s or debt. If the government did print dollars, instead of borrowing them from a privately-owned central bank that prints them, Uncle Sam would not have an eleven trillion dollar millstone hanging around his neck. As Thomas Edison astutely observed:

"If our nation can issue a dollar bond, it can issue a dollar bill. The element that makes the bond good, makes the bill good, also. The difference between the bond and the bill is that the bond lets money brokers collect twice the amount of the bond and an additional 20%, whereas the currency pays nobody but those who contribute directly in some useful way.

It is absurd to say that our country can issue $30 million in bonds and not $30 million in currency. Both are promises to pay, but one promise fattens the usurers and the other helps the people."

A Wake-up Call

Henry Ford observed at about the same time:

"It is well enough that people of the nation do not understand our banking and monetary system, for if they did, I believe there would be a revolution before tomorrow morning."

Today we the people are starting to understand our banking and monetary system, and we are shocked, dismayed, and furious at what we are discovering. The wizard behind the curtain turns out to be a small group of men pulling levers and dials, creating an illusory money scheme that, behind all the talk and bravado, is mere smoke and mirrors. These levers are controlled by a privately-owned, unaccountable central bank called the Federal Reserve, which has recently dispensed billions if not trillions in funds to its banker cronies, without revealing where these monies are going even under Congressional inquiry or in response to Freedom of Information Act (FOIA) requests. As Chris Powell pointed out recently in conjunction with an FOIA request brought by Bloomberg News, which the Fed declined to comply with:

"Any government that can disburse $2 trillion secretly, without any accountability, is not a democratic government. It is government of, by, and, for the bankers."4

There was a time when private central bankers were the heavyweights in control, able to run their ultra-secret agenda with impunity; but that era is coming to an end. The bankers are scrambling, trying to patch up their crumbling creations with schemes, bailouts and sleight of hand. That effort, however, must ultimately prove futile. As investment adviser Rolfe Winkler said in a recent article:

"The great Ponzi scheme that is the Western World's economy has grown so big there's simply no 'fixing' it. Flushing more debt through the system would be like giving Madoff a few billion to tide him over. Or like adding another floor to the Tower of Babel. To what end? The collapse is already here. The question is: How much do we want it to hurt? Using the public's purse to finance 'confidence' in a system that is already kaput may delay the Day of Reckoning, sure, but at the cost of multiplying our losses. Perhaps fantastically."5

The bankers are on the run, feverishly trying to use the collapse of the current system to steer us toward an "Amero"-style North American currency, or a one-world private banking system and privately-issued global currency that they and only they control. We the people will not accept those solutions, however, no matter how bad things get. We demand real solutions that empower us, not further enslave us.

Abraham Lincoln had such a solution. President Obama, you can finally bring his monetary solution to fruition. Manifest the vision of Lincoln, Jefferson, Madison and Franklin, and we the people will make sure you are placed in the pantheon of our greatest leaders and are revered for all time. America's greatest days can still be ahead of us; but for this to happen, we need to expose and root out the deceptive banking scheme that would enslave us to a future of debt and increasing homelessness in this great country our forefathers founded. The time has come for democracy to rise superior to a private banking cartel and take back the power to create money once again. Such a transformation would represent the most epochal and empowering shift that humanity has ever seen. As you recently said:

"This country has never responded to a crisis by sitting on the sidelines and hoping for the best. Throughout our history we have met every great challenge with bold action and big ideas."

Your words are a timely reminder of our long legacy of action and bold solutions in the face of adversity. Can we do this? Yes we can.

Originally posted on Yes! Magazine Online
April 7, 2009.

For more information, see the writings of a variety of money reformers including David Korten, Richard Cook, Stephen Zarlenga, Michael Hudson and this author; articles collected at www.webofdebt.com/articles and www.GlobalResearch.ca; the documentary videos "The Money Masters" and "Money as Debt;" and proposed legislation by Congressman Dennis Kucinich to nationalize the Fed, and by Congressman Ron Paul to audit it (HR 1027).

Ellen Brown developed her research skills as an attorney practicing civil litigation in Los Angeles. In Web of Debt, her latest book, she turns those skills to an analysis of the Federal Reserve and "the money trust." She shows how this private cartel has usurped the power to create money from the people themselves, and how we the people can get it back. Her earlier books focused on the pharmaceutical cartel that gets its power from "the money trust." Her eleven books include Forbidden Medicine, Nature's Pharmacy (co-authored with Dr. Lynne Walker), and The Key to Ultimate Health (co-authored with Dr. Richard Hansen). Her websites are www.webofdebt.com and www.ellenbrown.com.

See Ellen Brown, "Borrowing from Peter to Pay Paul: The Wall Street Ponzi Scheme Called Fractional Reserve Banking," www.webofdebt.com/articles (December 29, 2008).

Congressman Charles Binderup in a 1941 speech, "How America Created Its Own Money in 1750: How Benjamin Franklin Made New England Prosperous."

Binderup quotes historian John Twells on this point.

E. Brown, "Turning the Tables on Wall Street: North Dakota Shows Cash-starved States How They Can Create Their Own Credit," www.webofdebt.com/articles (March 11, 2009).

Chris Powell, "Fed Refuses to Disclose Recipients of $2 Trillion," GATA (December 12, 2008).

Rolfe Winkler, "More Debt Won't Rescue the Great American Ponzi," Option Armageddon (March 9, 2009).

Special thanks to CC for his invaluable help with this article.

Author's Biography

The author, Charles Layne, was born and raised on a family farm in rural Hanover County, VA. After graduating from Beaver Dam High School in 1948 he attended Randolph-Macon College, a liberal arts institution in Ashland, VA., earning a degree in mathematics in 1952 He spent a career in high technology research and development in government laboratories and in the private sector. His work involved systems engineering and electro-optical technologies. Following an early retirement at fifty-five, he consulted for a few years before becoming a serious retiree.

This is the author's second book. In his first book, **"Memories of a Beaverdam Boy"**, he traces his life experiences from a rural family farm in Virginia through an exciting career in high technology work to a retirement activity of supporting a needy family in Liberia and young people in colleges in the Philippines.

This book, **"What You Need to Know About Taxes"**, is an outgrowth of a decade's long avocational study of monetary systems and the fiscal affairs of nations.
He currently lives in rural Virginia on the old family farm.

Note Regarding Software:

The results of two software programs have been used extensively in this book. By purchasing this book you are entitled to copies of these programs. Send a copy of your receipt for purchasing the book to:

flfirst500@aol.com

to receive the programs by return email.

The two software programs are available separately for $19.50.